College Reading Skills

Topics for the Restless, Book Three
Stimulating Selections for Indifferent Readers
Second Edition

Edward Spargo, Editor

Books in the Series:
Book One   Book Three
Book Two   Book Four

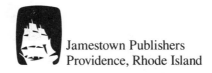

Jamestown Publishers
Providence, Rhode Island

Topics for the Restless, Book Three

Second Edition

Catalog No. 833

Cover and text design by Deborah Hulsey Christie

Cover credit: Copyright the Estate of Georgia O'Keeffe, 1961.

Inside Front Cover: UPI/BETTMAN NEWSPHOTOS
2 Travels with Ichabod: IPA/The Image Works
3 The Exercise Fix: Copyright 1983 David Stoecklein/The Stock Solution
4 Preserving Freedom of the Press: UPI/BETTMANN NEWSPHOTOS
5 Lincoln's Last Day: Library of Congress
6 Winning the Battle of the Bug, I: ©John Kohout/Root Resources
7 Winning the Battle of the Bug, II: Dan J. McCoy/Rainbow
8 Death with Dignity: ©Chuck Beckley/Southern Light
9 Something's Happening Out There: © 1983 CBS Inc. All Rights Reserved.
10 Tell-Tale Stones, Old Bones: Mary A. Root/Root Resources
11 The Great American Vandal: © 1988 Joseph V. DiChello Jr.
12 The Day Man First Flew: Smithsonian Institution Photo No. A-26767-B-2
13 Preserving Alaska's Prehistory: Alaska Division of Tourism
14 Hiroshima—Death and Rebirth, I: AP/WIDE WORLD PHOTOS
15 Hiroshima—Death and Rebirth, II: AP/WIDE WORLD PHOTOS
16 The Peter Principle: Illustration by Rich Bishop
17 The Return of the Salmon: © 1988 George Robbins Photo
18 The Fight to Stop Torture: Photo courtesy of Amnesty International
19 VD for the Millions: David & Linda Phillips
20 The Evidence Store: Jeff Greenberg

Printed in the United States   HS
91 92 93 94 95 7 6 5 4 3   7 6 5 4 3 2

ISBN: 0-89061-529-2

Readability			
Book One	F–G	Book Three	J–K
Book Two	H–I	Book Four	L–up

Acknowledgments

Acknowledgment is gratefully made to the following publishers and authors for permission to reprint these selections.

Travels with Ichabod by Eva Diamond. From *Motorland,* magazine of the California State Automobile Association. Copyright © 1972 by Eva Diamond. Reprinted by permission of the author.

The Exercise Fix by Eleanor Grant. Copyright © 1988 by the American Psychological Association. Reprinted with permission from *Psychology Today* magazine.

Preserving Freedom of the Press by Mario M. Cuomo. Reprinted from *USA Today* magazine, January 1986. Copyright © 1986 by the Society for the Advancement of Education.

Winning the Battle of the Bug, I, II by William Shelton. From *Exxon USA,* quarterly magazine of the Exxon Company. Reprinted with their permission.

Something's Happening Out There by Charles Kuralt. From *Family Circle* magazine, January 1973. Reprinted with their permission.

Tell-Tale Stones, Old Bones by Walter Olesky. Reprinted from *Marathon World,* published by Marathon Oil Company.

The Great American Vandal by John Keats. Copyright © 1972 by John Keats. Reprinted from Travel & Leisure. Copyright © 1972 by the American Express Publishing Corporation. Reprinted by permission of The Sterling Lord Agency, Inc.

Preserving Alaska's Prehistory by Downs Matthews. From *Exxon USA,* quarterly magazine of the Exxon Company. Reprinted with their permission.

Hiroshima—Death and Rebirth, I, II by C. E. Maine. From *50 True Tales of Terror,* edited by John Canning. Copyright © 1972 by Century Books, Ltd.

The Peter Principle. From *The Peter Principle* by Dr. Lawrence J. Peter and Raymond Hull. Copyright © 1969 by William Morrow & Company. Reprinted by permission of William Morrow & Company, Inc.

Contents

1 | Introductory Selection

*Explains How the Text is Organized and
How to Use It to Maximum Advantage*

Vocabulary—The five words below are from the story you are about to read. Study the words and their meanings. Then complete the ten sentences that follow, using one of the five words to fill in the blank in each sentence. Mark your answer by writing the letter of the word on the line before the sentence. Check your answers in the Answer Key on page 106.

A. intent: purpose

B. distribution: arrangement; organization

C. consecutively: in order; one after another

D. corresponding: matching

E. efficient: performing a task easily and skillfully

_____ 1. A wide _____ of topics is needed in order to appeal to all readers.

_____ 2. If you read each chapter _____ , you will understand the lessons more easily.

_____ 3. As you work through each selection, you will become more _____ at analyzing written material.

_____ 4. After finishing the book, you will have a good grasp of its _____ .

_____ 5. The skilled reader has learned that each kind of reading matter demands a _____ reading technique.

_____ 6. The exercises cover a wide _____ of reading and study skills.

_____ 7. In order to be an _____ reader, you must sharpen your critical reading skills.

_____ 8. To communicate with their readers is the _____ of all authors.

_____ 9. Answer the vocabulary questions by writing the letter _____ to the correct word.

_____ 10. Answer the questions _____ , and then turn to the answer key to correct your work.

(Before you begin reading this selection, turn to page 8 and record the hours and minutes in the box labeled *Starting Time* at the bottom of the second column. If you are using this text in class and your instructor has made provisions for timing, you need not stop now; read on.)

You are using this text for two purposes: (1) to improve your reading skills, and (2) to read articles and selections designed to make you think. Not every selection will be so demanding, however; many articles were chosen just for pure reading pleasure and enjoyment.

These selections span the range of human experience. It was the intent of the editor to find and include writings which show the real world, the world we all have to face daily. On these pages you will read and learn about current problems facing our society: the use of alcohol and other drugs, the struggle of women for recognition and independence, the seemingly unsolvable problem of disposing of garbage and other wastes of industrial production.

Many selections deal with the quality of our environment and possible new life-styles we may be forced to adopt in the future unless we deal now with air and water pollution, population growth, supplying food needs, caring for the homeless and aged with dignity and respect.

However, many selections treat some of the more pleasant concerns of today's older and more mature student. And finally, some selections just make for enjoyable reading.

Do not expect every selection to be equally interesting to you. In such a wide distribution of subject matter there are bound to be stories which will turn you on, but turn others off. Selections which may bore you, and therefore be hard to read and understand, may very well spark the interest of another reader.

A serious student, therefore, will approach each selection in this text with equal enthusiasm and a determination to succeed. This is the kind of attitude to develop toward reading—an attitude which will serve you well for the rest of your life.

The other purpose for using this text, that of reading and study improvement, recognizes reality, too: the reality of today. This text will help you to develop skills and techniques necessary for efficiency in our society.

Included in each selection are two Study Skills exercises. In these, you will learn methods of understanding, critical thinking skills, techniques of comprehension, and many other key ways to improve your reading ability. Both Study Skills exercises are designed to assist you in developing efficient reading techniques. As you read the selections in this book, you will find that often one Study Skills exercise leads directly to the next. It is important to read

> *It was the intent of the editor to find and include writings which show the real world, the world we all have to face daily.*

and work the Study Skills exercises consecutively in order to understand fully each subject.

Today's reader must be flexible enough to choose from a supply of skills one that is suitable for each reading task. The skilled reader has learned that each kind of reading matter demands a corresponding reading technique—there is no single "best" way to read. As you complete the selections and exercises in this book, you will find yourself growing in technique.

Using the Text

The twenty selections are designed to be read in numerical order, starting with the Introductory Selection and ending with Selection 20. Because the selections increase in difficulty as you progress through the book, the earlier ones prepare you to handle successfully the upcoming ones.

Here are the procedures to follow for reading each selection.

1. Answer the Vocabulary Questions. Immediately preceding each selection is a vocabulary previewing exercise. The exercise includes five vocabulary words from the selection, their meanings, and ten fill-in-the-blank sentences. To complete each sentence you will fill in the blank with one of the five vocabulary words.

Previewing the vocabulary in such a fashion will give you a head start on understanding the words when you encounter them in the selection. The fill-in-the-blank sentences present each word in context (surrounding words). That provides you with the chance to improve your ability to use context as an aid in understanding words. The efficient use of context is a valuable vocabulary tool.

After you have filled in the blanks in all ten sentences, check your answers in the Answer Key that starts on page 106. Be sure you understand the correct meaning of any wrong answers.

2. Preview before Reading. Previewing acquaints you with the overall content and structure of the selection before you actually read. It is like consulting a road map before taking a trip: planning the route gives you more confidence as you proceed and, perhaps, helps you avoid any unnecessary delays. Previewing should take about a minute or two and is done in this way:

a) Read the Title. Learn the writer's subject and, possibly, his point of view on it.

b) Read the Opening and Closing Paragraphs. These contain the introductory and concluding remarks. Important information is frequently presented in these key paragraphs.

c) Skim through. Try to discover the author's approach

to his subject. Does he use many examples? Is his purpose to sell you his ideas? What else can you learn now to help you when you read?

3. *Read the Selection.* Do not try to race through. Read well and carefully enough so that you can answer the comprehension questions that follow.

Keep track of your reading time by noting when you start and finish. A table on page 110 converts your reading time to a words-per-minute rate. Select the time from the table that is closest to your reading time. Record those figures in the boxes at the end of the selection. There is no one ideal reading speed for everything. The efficient reader varies his speed as the selection requires.

Many selections include a brief biography. Do not include this in your reading time. It is there to introduce you to the writer. Many of the selections have been reprinted from full-length books and novels. If you find a particular selection interesting, you may enjoy reading the entire book.

4. *Answer the Comprehension Questions.* After you have read the selection, find the comprehension questions that follow. These have been included to test your understanding of what you have read. The questions are diagnostic, too. Because the comprehension skill being measured is identified, you can detect your areas of weakness.

Read each question carefully and, without looking back, select one of the four choices given that answers that question most accurately or most completely. Frequently all four choices, or options, given for a question are *correct*, but one is the *best* answer. For this reason the comprehension questions are highly challenging and require you to be highly discriminating. You may, from time to time, disagree with the choice given in the Answer Key. When this happens, you have an opportunity to sharpen your powers of discrimination. Study the question again and seek to discover why the listed answer may be best. When you disagree with the text, you are thinking; when you objectively analyze and recognize your errors, you are learning.

The Answer Key begins on page 106. Find the answers for your selection and correct your comprehension work. When you discover a wrong answer, circle it and check the correct one.

The boxes following each selection contain space for your comprehension and vocabulary scores. Each correct vocabulary item is worth ten points and each correct comprehension answer is worth ten points.

Pages 111 and 112 contain graphs to be used for plotting your scores and tallying your incorrect responses.

On page 111 record your comprehension score at the appropriate intersection of lines, using an *X*. Use a circle, or some other mark, on the same graph to record your vocabulary results. Some students prefer to use different color inks, or pencil and ink, to distinguish between comprehension and vocabulary plottings.

On page 112 darken in the squares to indicate the comprehension questions you have missed. By referring to the Skills Profile as you progress through the text, you and your instructor will be able to tell which questions give you the most trouble. As soon as you detect a specific weakness in comprehension, consult with your instructor to see what supplementary materials he or she can provide or suggest.

A profitable habit for you to acquire is the practice of analyzing the questions you have answered incorrectly. If time permits, return to the selection to find and underline the passages containing the correct answers. This helps you to see what you missed the first time. Some interpretive and generalization type questions are not answered specifically in the text. In these cases bracket that part of the selection that alludes to the correct answer. Your instructor may recommend that you complete this step outside of class as homework.

5. *Complete the Study Skills Exercises.* Following the comprehension questions in each chapter is a passage on study skills. Some of the sentences in the passage have blanks where words have been omitted. Next to the passage are groups of five words, one group for each blank. Your task is to complete the passage by selecting the correct word for each of the blanks.

Next are five completion questions to be answered after you have reread the study skills passage.

The same answer key you have been using gives the correct responses for these two study skills exercises.

If class time is at a premium, your instructor may prefer that you complete the exercises out of class.

The following selections in this text are structured just like this introductory one. Having completed this selection and its exercises, you will then be prepared to proceed to Selection 2.

Starting Time		*Finishing Time*	
Reading Time		*Reading Rate*	
Comprehension		*Vocabulary*	

Comprehension — Read the following questions and statements. For each one, put an *x* in the box before the option that contains the most complete or accurate answer. Check your answers in the Answer Key on page 106.

1. How much time should you devote to previewing a selection?
   - ☐ a. Your time will vary with each selection.
   - ☐ b. You should devote about one or two minutes to previewing.
   - ☐ c. No specific time is suggested.
   - ☐ d. None—the instructor times the selection.

2. The way that the vocabulary exercises are described suggests that
   - ☐ a. the meaning of a word often depends on how it is used.
   - ☐ b. the final authority for word meaning is the dictionary.
   - ☐ c. words have precise and permanent meanings.
   - ☐ d. certain words are always difficult to understand.

3. The writer of this passage presents the facts in order of
   - ☐ a. importance.
   - ☐ b. purpose.
   - ☐ c. time.
   - ☐ d. operation.

4. *Topics for the Restless* is based on which of the following premises?
   - ☐ a. All students are restless.
   - ☐ b. Some students learn best when they are restless.
   - ☐ c. Writings dealing with real problems and situations should interest many students.
   - ☐ d. All of the selections in this text should interest all students.

5. How does the writer feel about reading speed?
   - ☐ a. It is a minimal aspect of the total reading situation.
   - ☐ b. It is second (following comprehension) in the ranking of skills.
   - ☐ c. It is connected to comprehension.
   - ☐ d. It should be developed at an early age.

6. The introductory selection
   - ☐ a. eliminates the need for oral instruction.
   - ☐ b. explains the proper use of the text in detail.
   - ☐ c. permits the student to learn by doing.
   - ☐ d. allows for variety and interest.

7. The introductory selection suggests that
   - ☐ a. most readers are not flexible.
   - ☐ b. students should learn to use different reading skills for different types of reading matter.
   - ☐ c. students today read better than students of the past did.
   - ☐ d. twenty selections is an ideal number for a reading improvement text.

8. The overall tone of this passage is
   - ☐ a. serious.
   - ☐ b. suspenseful.
   - ☐ c. humorous.
   - ☐ d. sarcastic.

9. The author of this selection is probably
   - ☐ a. a doctor.
   - ☐ b. an accountant.
   - ☐ c. an educator.
   - ☐ d. a businessman.

10. The writer of this passage makes his point clear by
   - ☐ a. telling a story.
   - ☐ b. listing historical facts.
   - ☐ c. using metaphors.
   - ☐ d. giving directions.

Comprehension Skills

1. recalling specific facts	6. making a judgment
2. retaining concepts	7. making an inference
3. organizing facts	8. recognizing tone
4. understanding the main idea	9. understanding characters
5. drawing a conclusion	10. appreciation of literary forms

Study Skills, Part One — Following is a passage with blanks where words have been omitted. Next to the passage are groups of five words, one group for each blank. Complete the passage by selecting the correct word for each of the blanks.

What Reading Is

Reading begins with the eyes. Before the mind can comprehend, the eyes must first apprehend. In other words, the net result of ___(1)___ words and understanding them is *reading*. In order to get the most benefit from a program

(1)   seeing   learning
    hearing   feeling   liking

of reading and study improvement, you should understand a little bit about how you see and recognize ___(2)___ when you read.

WHAT THE EYES SEE, I

1. Eye Fixations. The eyes do not move smoothly across a printed line, although to a good reader, it may seem as if they do. The eyes move in jerks, making stop-and-go movements along the lines of ___(3)___ . The stops are called fixations, and only during these stops do you actually read. Your eyes move too quickly between fixations for any clear vision; they must stop, or fixate, in order to read words.

When you read, 90 to 95 percent of your time is spent fixating. The movement from one stop to the next is extremely ___(4)___ , taking less than ¹/₄₀ of a second in normal reading. This happens so quickly that you are usually unaware of anything but a ___(5)___ movement of your eyes across the page.

2. Return Sweep. At the end of each line, your eyes make a return sweep to the beginning of the next line. This motion is also rapid, usually taking less than ¹/₂₀ of a second, and must be done accurately for efficient reading. ___(6)___ return sweeps occur when the eyes return to the beginning of the same line, when they skip a line, or when they miss the beginning of the next line.

3. Regressions. Sometimes your eyes move back for a second look at something you've already read. These movements are called regressions. Your eyes tend to regress when a word is ___(7)___ the first time or when the meaning of a word or phrase is not clear.

(2)		
ideas	words	
relationships	characters	emotions

(3)		
fixations	print	
thought	notes	inquiry

(4)		
important	slow	
difficult	rapid	painful

(5)		
continued	practiced	
jerky	advanced	smooth

(6)		
Successful	Numerous	
Favorable	Inaccurate	Unnecessary

(7)		
reorganized	enjoyed	
missed	rejected	unknown

Study Skills, Part Two—Read the study skills passage again, paying special attention to the lesson being taught. Then, without looking back at the passage, complete each sentence below by writing in the missing word or words. Check the Answer Key on page 106 for the answers to Study Skills, Part One, and Study Skills, Part Two.

1. Seeing words and understanding them results in _____ .

2. Actual reading takes place when the eye stops and _____ occurs.

3. The movement between stops is so rapid that the reader is _____ of it.

4. At the end of each line, the eye makes a return sweep to the _____ of the next line.

5. The return movements made to reconsider words are called _____ .

2 | Travels with Ichabod

by Eva Diamond

Vocabulary—The five words below are from the story you are about to read. Study the words and their meanings. Then complete the ten sentences that follow, using one of the five words to fill in the blank in each sentence. Mark your answer by writing the letter of the word on the line before the sentence. Check your answers in the Answer Key on page 106.

A. tooled: drove

B. rendered: made

C. itinerary: record of travel; schedule

D. elusive: difficult to find or attain

E. ensconced: settled comfortably or securely

_____ 1. Some people use a detailed _____ when they travel.

_____ 2. The author spent many nights happily _____ in Ichabod's bed.

_____ 3. Laundromats apparently proved _____ in many parts of Europe.

_____ 4. The author and her family _____ along many back roads in Europe.

_____ 5. The high cost of hotels _____ the author's original plan of a Grand Tour impractical.

_____ 6. One advantage of camping is that a traveler's _____ can be quite flexible.

_____ 7. The author discovered many idyllic spots as she _____ around Europe.

_____ 8. Each night the author's daughter found herself _____ in the hammock in Ichabod's pop-top.

_____ 9. The author searched for those _____ campgrounds where the washing machines worked and the showers sprayed hot water.

_____ 10. Sometimes the showers at campgrounds were _____ useless by faulty equipment or broken controls.

The little red van turned us into first-class gypsies overnight.

As one who viewed a sleep-out with the Camp Fire Girls as a mortification of the flesh, I brushed off camping trips through Europe as showy masochism. Moreover, sleeping bags, camping gas, and privies did not jibe with my dream of the Grand Tour.

But that was before I knew Ichabod, the jolly little red van that tooled us so joyously from castle to camping platz, and turned us into first-class gypsies almost overnight.

We were plotting a nice three month rented-car-cozy-inn tour when we discovered that European inflation had devalued us to backpacks with no youth travel advantages, physical or monetary. So we got a *European Camping Atlas* and reluctantly ordered Ichabod, a Volkswagen pop-top campmobile, to be picked up in Germany, used, and shipped home.

It was not love at first sight with Ichabod and me. Squatting on its launching pad at the Wiedenbreuck factory, he resembled a plastic pug dog, with beady eyes, flat nose, and a bumper mouth drooling in the afternoon drizzle. I wanted to growl at him, but was restrained by my husband's smile as he patted the beast's haunches, and by the ecstatic face on our 11-year-old daughter, already playing stewardess at Ichabod's toy sink.

When I pointed out that there would be no room for me inside "that bread wagon" once our suitcases were unpacked, the captain and stewardess banished me to the factory store with a handful of funny money and orders to equip Ichabod.

As the store clerk did not speak English and I did not understand about money or camping gas, it was a grueling encounter. Eventually, though, I returned to Ichabod with stove, bottled gas, pots, pans, towels, dishes, and sleeping bags, only to be sent off again to furnish the larder at a store that seemed to deal mostly in sausage. This time when I returned, I found to my surprise that little old Ichabod had swallowed a mountain of luggage, clothing, and camping gear. And the groceries went into the cupboards with space to spare.

We climbed aboard and started out through the rain. Ichabod's height was enough to make me feel like a trucker's moll, but those extra inches also increased visibility, and what we saw on takeoff made our spirits soar. The brick and timber village, the Gothic church with its ancient stones blue and green with age, and the hyacinths. Travel with Ichabod had possibilities.

But those possibilities were diminished when we returned at dusk to the factory camping platz to cook our sausage and bed down for the night. Ichabod's top popped properly, and the table came into place nicely, but the captain had trouble assembling the stove. First, because it was dark. Second, because the directions were in German. We ate crackers in the blackness and fumbled to get the table folded up and the beds down. The stewardess swung neatly into her hammock in the pop-top, but getting into our "big bed" was like slithering into a half-opened sardine can. And it was cold that night. (The captain insisted that our sleeping bags did not zip together, and only in Greece did I discover that they did.) It was noisy, too, with the rain on our metal roof, wind in our pop-top, and *TRUCKS*.

But in the morning the magic returned with heavenly villages and spring countryside, lunch in a woods near a tile-pink town suspended between misty blue mountains and misty blue lake. Then Marberg Cathedral with spooky sarcophagi, the castle where Martin Luther changed the world, and a store where we bought winter pajamas and ski slacks.

However, we had lingered too long. We raced the darkness to Frankfurt, site of our projected camp, encountering detours which rendered useless all our maps. The captain got tense, the stewardess wept, and I, the navigator, got shrill during the two hours we fought our way through the city in search of the platz, which looked like a San Joaquin Valley fruit camp in a January flood.

But the next day we had sun, sparkling rivers, Heidelberg, and better luck with our camp. We couldn't find one. We had left the highway and followed the international camping signs until they disappeared in snow and darkness. Turning around, we became so lost we couldn't even find the highway. So we just drove Ichabod into some bushes, heated soup, and slept.

So we were learning about camping—the hard way. Soon we had set a simple policy: check camping guide for first-class camps, check months camps are open, do not hunt for camps after dark, and park level. After a shattering experience when two dark figures rose out of the night and tried to enter Ichabod, we also ruled only to stop in established, operating camps.

By Austria, we were finding camps with hot showers, washing machines, and restaurants with strolling violinists. I began to see camping as freedom—freedom to roam without reservations, without schedules, and without lugging luggage. And we could camp for a week for the price of one day of using a hotel and restaurants.

There are hundreds of camps in Europe, some the Hiltons of camping and some the flophouses. Usually, the best and most numerous are located in recreational areas used by Europeans—along lakes, oceans, or rivers. We found the Swiss camps to be consistently good, beautifully situated, and sparkling clean. Camping in France was fine, too, but there we had to seek our spots, as some French camps can be grubby. Luckily, an

Englishwoman we camped near in Siena gave us the map and brochure for French chateau camps—all located off main roads at idyllic old mansions whose present owners had installed camping facilities. Some of these camps are listed in the *Camping Atlas,* but not as chateau camps.

In England and Scotland, our camps were trailer parks, usually located on farms. Only once did we have to dodge cows, but the mountain stream and ancient stone farmhouse were so lovely that we didn't mind. Besides our child was fascinated by the primitive dairy operation with a whole family of children working.

In Italy, Germany, and Austria, we had to choose camps carefully, often building our itinerary around the first class camps and saving the risks for places where we had no choice. Greece offered relatively few camps and little hot water, but we had glorious sea bathing in cool, blue water. Actually, our favorite camp was in Greece. It was a Garden of Eden in Corfu, where Ichabod relaxed in grandeur with ancient olives twisting over his pop-top and carpets of wild flowers dancing at his tires. And the camp beach adjoined Club Mediterranee.

We came to love camping with Ichabod. Surely, this is the only way to travel with children. After a day of museums or driving, our little girl would race around the meadows doing flips for an hour.

Naturally, there were inconveniences. Showers, for example: always tempting, always elusive. Often as not, no hot water was promised. Or we'd have to chase around after mysterious coins, slugs, keys, or secret codes, only to be cheated by faulty equipment or scalded by sprays with no controls.

Laundry was a nuisance, too. Not the washing—the drying, which just doesn't happen in rainy Europe. Poor Ichabod often got so steamed up with wet laundry that we could hardly see out. But we reminded ourselves that damp socks soften callouses, and shabby clothes ward off persons trying to sell gold watches. And a wagon load of wet laundry is marvelous for crossing international borders. Customs men searched other cars diligently, but one glance at Ichabod and we were waved through.

As the time and miles and castles rolled by and the laundry got damper, Ichabod's crew laughed more and sang more, and took what came as high adventure. As the silly bonds of our comfort-oriented civilization loosened, we came to know the real fun of camping throughout Europe—meeting other campers. The platzes were friendly places, where common purpose and common plumbing transcended national differences and brought people together.

Only in glamour capitals did my enthusiasm for camping wane. Something about crawling out of a hippie van to do Paris or Rome seemed slightly shabby, but even that was of small importance. We enjoyed our travels with Ichabod right down to our last night on a pig farm called "Toad's Acres," right outside Cambridge.

At the end of our journey, when we were safely ensconced in a pleasant London hotel and Ichabod was abandoned to a shipping garage, we truly missed camping. We resented the added expense of hoteling, and we resented the time wasted as we yielded to temptation and lounged around the hotel room. Ichabod's staunch captain spent extra hours snoring in the big, soft bed. Our lively little stewardess was forever sprawled on the carpet, absorbing the horrors of the London tabloids, while I stagnated in the hot water bathtub.

That's no way to see Europe. I'll take Ichabod any day.

Starting Time		Finishing Time	
Reading Time		Reading Rate	
Comprehension		Vocabulary	

Comprehension— Read the following questions and statements. For each one, put an *x* in the box before the option that contains the most complete or accurate answer. Check your answers in the Answer Key on page 106.

1. The best campsites are those used by the
   - ☐ a. wealthy.
   - ☐ b. tourists.
   - ☐ c. Europeans.
   - ☐ d. military.

2. The quality of campgrounds in Europe
   - ☐ a. varies tremendously.
   - ☐ b. is uniformly good.
   - ☐ c. changes with the weather.
   - ☐ d. usually disappoints Americans.

3. Which of the following was not part of the Diamonds' camping policy?
   - ☐ a. Check camping guide for first-class camps.
   - ☐ b. Stop only in camps with shower facilities.
   - ☐ c. Do not hunt for camps after dark.
   - ☐ d. Stop only in established, operating camps.

4. The author's main point can be expressed by which of the following?
   - ☐ a. Adaptability and a capacity to enjoy simple pleasures are vital to campers.
   - ☐ b. Overland travel should never be undertaken without an experienced guide.
   - ☐ c. The secret of successful camping is a well-provisioned van.
   - ☐ d. Camping grounds in Europe are generally unsanitary and unsafe.

5. The first night spent aboard Ichabod was a
   - ☐ a. disappointing experience.
   - ☐ b. relaxing change of pace.
   - ☐ c. unbearable episode.
   - ☐ d. dangerous experience.

6. The author's daughter was
   - ☐ a. unhappy during most of the trip.
   - ☐ b. a nuisance to her parents.
   - ☐ c. a natural camper.
   - ☐ d. in need of more companionship.

7. The two shopping trips the author made to provision Ichabod were
   - ☐ a. extremely frustrating.
   - ☐ b. obviously unsuccessful.
   - ☐ c. unnecessarily expensive.
   - ☐ d. educational experiences.

8. The author describes the European countryside
   - ☐ a. in glowing terms.
   - ☐ b. in a despairing tone.
   - ☐ c. with obvious disappointment.
   - ☐ d. with artificial enthusiasm.

9. The author could best be described as
   - ☐ a. easygoing.
   - ☐ b. close-minded.
   - ☐ c. opinionated.
   - ☐ d. grumpy.

10. The author's treatment of Ichabod is an example of
   - ☐ a. simile.
   - ☐ b. metaphor.
   - ☐ c. hyperbole.
   - ☐ d. personification.

Comprehension Skills

1. recalling specific facts	6. making a judgment
2. retaining concepts	7. making an inference
3. organizing facts	8. recognizing tone
4. understanding the main idea	9. understanding characters
5. drawing a conclusion	10. appreciation of literary forms

Study Skills, Part One—Following is a passage with blanks where words have been omitted. Next to the passage are groups of five words, one group for each blank. Complete the passage by selecting the correct word for each of the blanks.

WHAT THE EYES SEE, II

In comparison studies of good and poor readers, the records consistently show that good readers make ___(1)___ fixations per line, since they see more words during each fixation, and make fewer regressions.

Eye movements, then, reveal certain characteristics of a reader's skill.

One study has shown that fairly good student readers average six fixations a line and one regression every two lines and that ¼ of a second is the average duration of each fixation.

Since the eye movements of good readers are known and are recognized as ___(2)___ of reading proficiency, visual training is often incorporated in reading improvement instruction. Its purpose is to teach students to enlarge the span of their fixations and improve the efficiency of eye movements.

However, the eyes will take in only as much as the mind

(1)   more   fewer
    even   good   inferior

(2)   indications   problems
    results   areas   inductions

can understand; so it is more ___(3)___ to think in terms of comprehension span. Just as important as pressing for shorter fixations and taking in greater gulps of words is the need for developing techniques that encourage reading for meaning. One way of doing this is to see words in thought groups by ___(4)___ words meaningfully when reading.

Eye-Voice Span. When you read aloud, your eyes normally read ahead of your voice. The number of words between a word being ___(5)___ and the word farthest along that can be seen at the same time makes up what is called the eye-voice span.

Good readers display a wide eye-voice span of about five words. Poor readers, on the other hand, possess a narrow span (one or two words) because they are reading word by word with little ___(6)___ of what is coming next. To see how important this concept is to efficient reading, listen to a child read and notice how difficult it is to understand.

Thus, the skills you develop in oral reading help you to read better ___(7)___ . Practice in increasing eye-voice span is practice in seeing word groups intelligently and using context as an aid to meaning.

| (3) | enjoyable | | interesting |
| | popular | durable | accurate |

| (4) | combining | | separating |
| | reading | compounding | considering |

| (5) | spelled | | scanned |
| | spoken | understood | selected |

| (6) | sense | | relation |
| | review | plan | care |

| (7) | painlessly | | naturally |
| | often | silently | effortlessly |

Study Skills, Part Two—Read the study skills passage again, paying special attention to the lesson being taught. Then, without looking back at the passage, complete each sentence below by writing in the missing word or words. Check the Answer Key on page 106 for the answers to Study Skills, Part One, and Study Skills, Part Two.

1. Good readers make fewer _____ or regressions per line.

2. Visual training is often included in reading _____ instruction.

3. Equal in importance to visual training is the encouragement of reading

    for _____ .

4. Eye-voice span is demonstrated in _____ reading.

5. Attempting to increase eye-voice span can help in using _____

    as an aid to meaning.

3 The Exercise Fix

by Eleanor Grant

Vocabulary—The five words below are from the story you are about to read. Study the words and their meanings. Then complete the ten sentences that follow, using one of the five words to fill in the blank in each sentence. Mark your answer by writing the letter of the word on the line before the sentence. Check your answers in the Answer Key on page 106.

A. tedium: boredom

B. irritant: something that annoys or exasperates

C. jeopardy: peril

D. invincible: incapable of being conquered

E. diversify: vary

_____ 1. Too much exercise can put a person's health in _____ .

_____ 2. "Runner's high" makes a person feel _____ .

_____ 3. Many non-athletes object to the _____ of running.

_____ 4. People who are addicted to exercise should try to _____ their activities.

_____ 5. An exercise addict may find warnings about over-training an _____ .

_____ 6. Exercise addicts usually have no desire to _____ their schedule.

_____ 7. Even the healthiest, best-trained athletes are not _____ when it comes to injuries.

_____ 8. In extreme cases, an addict's commitment to exercise can put her or his personal relationships in _____ .

_____ 9. Real exercise zealots do not mind the _____ of running around a track or biking on a stationary bike.

_____ 10. For some, losing a day of exercise is an _____ .

THE STOCK SOLUTION

"If I don't run, I feel like a slob: lazy, heavy, and tired. Running is my life. It makes me feel like a complete person, and I need to do it every day."

The long winter months take a heavy toll on the recreational athlete. Many let their running shoes gather dust in closets or allow their bicycles to lean dejectedly against cellar walls. They resign themselves to watching their sleek lines grow softer, and some may even be grateful for the rest.

There are others, however, who brave the slush-locked streets or the grinding tedium of laps on an indoor track rather than miss their daily dose of exercise. For them, a day off is an irritant, a missed week is a severe trial, and a month off is a life crisis of catastrophic proportions. They are people such as Richard, an executive in his early 30s who found himself unable to give up his daily seven- to eight-mile run, even though it interfered with his job and made strangers of his children. "When I run, I feel very energized, proud of myself, and have more confidence," Richard says. "If I don't run, I feel like a slob: lazy, heavy, and tired. I won't last long at my job if I don't spend the necessary hours there, but if I don't run I won't be very good at it either. . . . Running is my life. It makes me feel like a complete person, and I need to do it every day." Richard is addicted to exercise.

Researchers have known of the addictive qualities of running and other aerobic sports for some time. At first exercise addiction seemed harmless, and many believed that it was beneficial. Psychiatrist William Glasser, who popularized the concept in his 1976 book *Positive Addiction,* contrasted compulsive running with the use of alcohol or drugs to cope with life's problems; running neither destroyed the mind nor pickled the liver, he argued, but instead strengthened both body and soul.

Soon, however, the focus shifted to the darker side of exercise addiction. In 1979, psychologist William Morgan found that addicted runners continued to run even when it put their jobs, their family relationships, and their health in jeopardy. This reinforced an observation made by many physicians and sports-medicine specialists: Some "recreational" athletes push themselves to the point of injuries such as shin splints or stress fractures, then refuse to rest and recuperate, causing greater and perhaps permanent damage.

The reason exercise addicts keep punishing themselves probably lies in what happens when they don't run, swim, bicycle, or work out. Connie Chan, a psychologist at the University of Massachusetts at Boston, has studied the psychological consequences of being unable to exercise. Chan and psychologist Hildy Y. Grossman compared 30 male and female runners who had been laid low by minor injuries for at least two weeks with a similar group who continued to run. Those who could not run displayed more signs of depression, anxiety, and confusion than did those who could, and they were far less happy with themselves and their bodies. Like other addictions, exercise appears to have withdrawal symptoms.

Chan has treated dozens of running addicts and has learned that they have some common characteristics. Addicts must run daily to function normally, and they become irritable, tense, and anxious if unable to exercise for a few days. These are the short-term symptoms of exercise withdrawal. When unable to run for longer periods of time, addicts can experience more drastic symptoms including depression, lack of energy, loss of interest in eating, sex, and other activities, decreased self-confidence and self-esteem, insomnia, and weight loss or gain. They continue to run while injured and organize their lives around exercise and related activities, ignoring their families and careers.

Edward Colt, an endocrinologist and former medical director of the New York City marathon, believes that exercise addiction is very widespread: "I think that all— 100 percent—of the people who exercise regularly are addicted to some extent." But not everyone agrees that the problem is so extensive; some, including Morgan, now question its very existence. Morgan no longer studies the issue: He feels that the concept of exercise addiction is extremely murky, and no one has ever confirmed that exercise is addictive in the same way that drugs and alcohol are.

One popular—but unproved—theory is that athletes become hooked on endorphins, the body's natural painkillers, which surge into the brain and the bloodstream during strenuous exercise. Colt and his colleagues have done studies that show runners do have elevated endorphin levels after exercise, but no one has demonstrated that these substances actually have physiologically addictive effects. It's more likely that the "runner's high" is a feeling of well-being that comes with release of pent-up stress.

Endorphins might contribute to exercise addiction, perhaps by dulling the pain of aching muscles or battered bones that would otherwise tell people that they are overdoing it, but Chan thinks that the roots of the problem run much deeper: For the addict, exercise fulfills profound psychological needs.

The typical addict is usually not a world-class athlete; more likely, he or she is one of millions who have taken up aerobic sport in adulthood as a way of getting in shape or losing weight. People who stick to an aerobic exercise regimen usually find themselves not only slimming down and firming up but also feeling more relaxed and better able to cope with stress.

Potential addicts develop a heady sense of control over their bodies and feel invincible when running. They are intense individuals whose jobs often do not produce quantifiable results, and in their increasing mileage and other "personal bests" they discover a source of measurable achievement. For many, these results are a revelation, a self-affirmation that helps to overcome deeply buried fears of powerlessness and personal inadequacy. Eventually, exercise becomes much more than a form of recreation or a path to physical fitness. It is the root of their psychological well-being, the touchstone of their identities.

Some exercise fanatics are single professionals who would rather hit the streets or the gym after work than confront an empty house. For some, workouts meet their needs for social contact; for others, exercising is a way to avoid thinking about an empty social calendar. For all, this heightens their sense of dependence on exercise.

Chan and Colt have found that many exercise addicts show a history of compulsive behavior. "In my experience, many [running addicts] are simply replacing one addiction with another," Colt says. "I've seen many former workaholics, alcoholics, gamblers, and smokers."

True to form, these addicts do not seek help willingly. "There's only one thing they want," says Colt, "and that is to find a doctor who will provide the magic cure that will allow them to keep running." Chan agrees, saying, "As long as they're able to run, [addicts] don't see a problem." Many of the exercise addicts whom Chan treats are referred to her by physicians, frustrated when their patients will not stop running long enough to let over-training injuries heal. By the time disabled runners reach her door, most are already deep in the throes of withdrawal and are more than a little bewildered by their symptoms.

"It's one thing to expect physical changes when you're not allowed to run, but exercise addicts are not prepared for the psychological repercussions," Chan says. "One of the things I offer them is reassurance that withdrawal is common and that they can get through it and get back in shape."

Chan knows the pangs of going without only too well. Eight years ago, while still in graduate school, stress fractures brought her 60-miles-per-week running regimen to an agonizing halt. At first, she tried to run through the pain. When she finally took her physician's advice and stopped running for several weeks, she found herself growing anxious and unable to concentrate. "I felt like I was falling apart," Chan says. "I was really preoccupied with the idea of running and racing, and with the thought that I'd never get back into competitive form. Of course, I knew it was irrational—you just don't get that out of shape in a few weeks." This extreme reaction was quite disturbing, she says, and came as a shock "to someone who thought she had a pretty balanced sense of herself."

Chan helps patients identify how they benefit from running psychologically, in terms of self-esteem and stress control, and explores with them other activities that might offer similar rewards. She often suggests joining a hiking club or pursuing educational interests. If an injury does not preclude all exercise, she encourages patients to walk, swim, or participate in whatever physical activity possible to minimize withdrawal and maintain some conditioning. To help patients cope with stress, Chan often tells them to relive a favorite run in their minds.

Once addicted athletes are physically well enough to start exercising again, Chan advises them to take it slow at first and diversify their physical activities, perhaps by taking up a sport that stresses a different set of muscles, tendons, and ligaments. They also need to become more involved with activities and people who are not connected to the exercise ritual.

Chan does not try to get people to give up exercise altogether: "I love to run. I would never tell anyone not to run." But with any exercise program, she says, moderation is the key to gaining the greatest benefits, both physical and psychological. Those who depend exclusively on one activity for a sense of well-being are flirting with addiction. In the long run, it doesn't work.

Starting Time			Finishing Time	
Reading Time			Reading Rate	
Comprehension			Vocabulary	

Comprehension — Read the following questions and statements. For each one, put an x in the box before the option that contains the most complete or accurate answer. Check your answers in the Answer Key on page 106.

1. Endorphins are
   □ a. responsible for "runner's high."
   □ b. the body's natural painkillers.
   □ c. muscle relaxants.
   □ d. effective remedies for exercise addiction.

2. Doctors Chan and Colt believe that many exercise addicts have
   □ a. addictive personalities.
   □ b. inadequate careers.
   □ c. low self-esteem.
   □ d. malfunctions in their endocrine systems.

3. Richard felt best when
   - ☐ a. being treated for shin splints.
   - ☐ b. working out at the gym.
   - ☐ c. running.
   - ☐ d. immersed in work.

4. Another title for this selection might be
   - ☐ a. "A Blessing in Disguise."
   - ☐ b. "Too Much of a Good Thing."
   - ☐ c. "New Solutions to Old Problems."
   - ☐ d. "Adding Insult to Injury."

5. Addiction to exercise
   - ☐ a. does not exist.
   - ☐ b. can be detrimental.
   - ☐ c. is as harmful as any other addiction.
   - ☐ d. is easily overcome.

6. Exercise enthusiasts should
   - ☐ a. learn to relax.
   - ☐ b. take long breaks between training periods.
   - ☐ c. consult a psychologist.
   - ☐ d. seek moderation.

7. Psychologist Connie Chan was once
   - ☐ a. an alcoholic.
   - ☐ b. an exercise addict.
   - ☐ c. married to an exercise addict.
   - ☐ d. a world-class athlete.

8. The overall tone of the selection is
   - ☐ a. lightly humorous.
   - ☐ b. gently mocking.
   - ☐ c. critical and disapproving.
   - ☐ d. reasoned and serious.

9. Exercise addicts are usually people who like to
   - ☐ a. dabble in new things.
   - ☐ b. be the center of attention.
   - ☐ c. socialize.
   - ☐ d. succeed.

10. The selection is written in the form of
    - ☐ a. a narrative.
    - ☐ b. a report.
    - ☐ c. a critique.
    - ☐ d. an interview.

Comprehension Skills

1. recalling specific facts	6. making a judgment
2. retaining concepts	7. making an inference
3. organizing facts	8. recognizing tone
4. understanding the main idea	9. understanding characters
5. drawing a conclusion	10. appreciation of literary forms

Study Skills, Part One—Following is a passage with blanks where words have been omitted. Next to the passage are groups of five words, one group for each blank. Complete the passage by selecting the correct word for each of the blanks.

Recognizing Words, I

Once you have seen the words, you must recognize or identify them before any ___(1)___ can take place. This involves association, which, in fact, is the way you first learned to read. We have to be taught to associate our response to a spoken word with that same word when it is ___(2)___ . Reading is a controlled form of listening, with print substituted for spoken words.

For this process to work in reading, the spoken word must mean something to us. A brand new ___(3)___ , or one that we don't recognize, won't mean anything to us written or spoken.

1. Phonics. When we are first taught to read, we learn to sound out words, and to pronounce them. Once we say the word, we then recognize it as a word we know. It is the discovery of the ___(4)___ of words that makes reading possible. Simply defined, phonics are the sounds given to words by their letters.

(1)   pronunciation   context
    involvement   appreciation   comprehension

(2)   transmitted   mentioned
    written   heard   observed

(3)   idea   word
    friend   alternative   concept

(4)   spelling   pronunciation
    appearance   sound   association

By the time you finish high school, you can probably recognize more than 50,000 words when you hear them. Using your knowledge of phonics, you can identify a __(5)__ word as one of these.

Your knowledge of phonics begins with the __(6)__ made by the vowels and consonants. Vowels give words their distinctive sounds, but they are not as __(7)__ to word recognition as the consonants. Try reading the following sentences with the consonants left out and then with the vowels left out.

(5)   different   recognized
   spoken   pronounced   printed

(6)   impressions   memories
   sounds   associations   announcements

(7)   relevant   harmful
   important   rewarding   confusing

Consonants omitted:
I_ i_ _o_ _a_ _ _o _ea_
_o_ _ _ _i _e _ _i_.

Vowels omitted:
_t _s n_t h_rd t_ r_ _d
w_rds l_k_ th_s.

Study Skills, Part Two—Read the study skills passage again, paying special attention to the lesson being taught. Then, without looking back at the passage, complete each sentence below by writing in the missing word or words. Check the Answer Key on page 106 for the answers to Study Skills, Part One, and Study Skills, Part Two.

1. Comprehension of words involves _____ .

2. Reading is a controlled form of _____ .

3. _____ are the sounds given to words by their letters.

4. Knowledge of how a word sounds enables you to identify it in _____ form.

5. Consonants are more important to word recognition than _____ .

4 | Preserving Freedom of the Press

by Mario M. Cuomo

Vocabulary—The five words below are from the story you are about to read. Study the words and their meanings. Then complete the ten sentences that follow, using one of the five words to fill in the blank in each sentence. Mark your answer by writing the letter of the word on the line before the sentence. Check your answers in the Answer Key on page 106.

A. ambiguous: unclear

B. incessantly: without pause

C. vitriol: abusive feelings or statements

D. provocative: likely to cause deep feelings

E. illustrious: renowned

_____ 1. Even the most _____ leaders of our country have been criticized by members of the press.

_____ 2. The press has worked _____ to expose corruption and abuse of power.

_____ 3. The Founding Fathers included in the Constitution the _____ claim to freedom of the press.

_____ 4. The _____ of presidents against the press is nothing new.

_____ 5. The Iranian arms deal raised _____ questions about the United States' foreign policy.

_____ 6. Such _____ presidents as Thomas Jefferson and Franklin Delano Roosevelt occasionally railed against the press.

_____ 7. In an effort to dodge the truth, some public officials give _____ answers to reporters' questions.

_____ 8. Public _____ against "pack journalism" and other questionable practices is leading the press to reexamine its techniques.

_____ 9. The Supreme Court works to hand down rulings which are not _____ .

_____ 10. Some people clamor _____ about the need for more restrictions on the press.

The more I learn about government and especially about democracy, the more deeply convinced I become that one of our greatest strengths as a people is our right to full and free expression. No people have benefited more from the gift of free speech and a free press. Never before in history has the gift been so generously given or so fully used. From the very launching of our nation, these freedoms were regarded as essential protections against official repression.

The Founding Fathers were convinced that much of the struggle for American freedom would be the struggle over a free press. So, they were careful to provide that the right

The Founding Fathers knew the dangers of a truly free press, but they demanded freedom of the press anyway.

of free expression, through a free press, would be preserved in their new nation, especially insofar as the press dealt with government and public officials. They declared that right of free expression in the First Amendment to the Constitution and wrote it in the simplest, least ambiguous language they could fashion: "Congress shall make no law respecting an establishment of religion, or prohibiting the free exercise thereof, or abridging the freedom of speech or of the press. . . ."

The Founding Fathers knew precisely what they were dealing with. The press of their time was not only guilty of bad taste and inaccuracy, it was partisan, reckless, sometimes vicious, and, indeed, the Founding Fathers were themselves often at the point end of the press sword.

In view of that experience, they might have written amendments that never mentioned freedom of the press, or they might have tried to protect against an imperfect press like the one they dealt with—with conditions, qualifications, requirements, and penalties—but they did not. They knew the dangers. They knew that broad freedoms inevitably would be accompanied by some abuse and even harm to innocent people. Knowing all the odds, they chose to gamble on liberty.

The gamble has made us all rich. Overall, the press has been a force for good—educating our people, guarding our freedom, watching our government—challenging it, goading it, revealing it, forcing it into the open. Teapot Dome, the Pentagon Papers, Watergate, even the recent revelations of corruption in New York City—these might never have occurred were it not for our free press. The press's insistence on forcing the White House to begin to tell the truth about the Iranian arms transaction is a recent dramatic reminder of how the press works incessantly to assure our liberty by guaranteeing our awareness. Less dramatically, the work of revelation by the press goes on day after day at all levels of government, all over the nation.

Surely, the preservation of this extraordinary strength is worth our eternal vigilance. That is why I believe it is appropriate to consider the matter of freedom of the

press now, at this moment. It appears to me—and to others as well—that we are approaching a time when shifts in our law may seriously dilute the protection of the press and thereby weaken the fabric of this society.

What is the public perception of the press today? Is it regarded as less than perfect? If so, how specifically?

It might be worth noting here that, in earlier times, many of our leading public officials were among the press's harshest critics. Today, the press is apt to refer to a public official who criticizes the media as "Nixonian." If, however, presidential labels are appropriate, the media might just as fairly call its critics "Washingtonian," "Jeffersonian," "Lincolnian," "Taftian," "Wilsonian," "Rooseveltian," "Kennedyesque," or "Johnsonian."

For example, George Washington called the press "infamous scribblers." Thomas Jefferson wrote: "Even the least informed of the people have learnt that nothing in a newspaper is to be believed."

Theodore Roosevelt added action to his vitriol. He had Joseph Pulitzer and his *New York World* indicted for criminal libel after the newspaper charged corruption in connection with the digging of the Panama Canal.

William Howard Taft found one paper so bad as to be "intolerable." He told his assistant not to show him *The New York Times.* "I don't think reading the *Times* will do me any good and would only be provocative in me of . . . anger and contemptuous feeling."

Woodrow Wilson lost his conciliatory disposition in dealing with the press. He said, "The real trouble is that the newspapers get the real facts but do not find them to their taste and do not use them as given them, and in some of the newspaper offices, news is deliberately invented."

Franklin Delano Roosevelt invented a Dunce Cap Club to which he would banish reporters whose questions annoyed him, and John F. Kennedy tore up all the White House subscriptions to *The Herald Tribune* because he did not think its coverage of him was fair.

The truth is that criticism of the press by its natural targets—public officials, governors, presidents—however illustrious, is not necessarily good evidence of the press's imperfection. Indeed, it can be argued that it is the best evidence of the press's effectiveness.

The press's job is to find the whole truth, especially that part of it which is forgotten, ignored, deliberately concealed, or distorted by public officials. The better the press does its job, the more likely future generations will be reading colorful condemnations of reporters and commentators by today's politicians, and the more likely that the historical record will be truthful and accurate.

I think I understand this as a public official myself.

Although I believe I have been treated very well by the press overall, from time to time I have had occasion to make my own criticisms of some members of the press and their coverage in particular cases. The response has revealed that politicians are not the only ones who are sensitive.

Of much more concern to the press than criticism from me and other public officials should be the criticism that comes from candid, thoughtful members of the press itself. Recently, it has been harsh indeed. What is worse is that the public at large appears to agree.

The press itself attributes much of this public disfavor to its own curable defects. Thus, "pack journalist" is a frequently heard complaint, citing the press's dependence on one another, forging a uniform point of view so as to avoid embarrassing differences, written as though every statement previously made by any reporter is indisputable, and the clannish locking of arms against critics from the outside. As Hodding Carter said in 1985, ". . . We are very, very good at pitching and very, very bad at catching. . . . The press appears to be paranoid when facing criticism itself."

Of course, there are times when a reporter's only reasonable access to important information requires that he or she assure the source of anonymity. The right to use that prerogative seems essential to effective reporting. However, another complaint frequently heard has to do with the press's excessive and unfairly exploitative use of unnamed, so-called confidential sources without checking their credentials, their motivation, or their reliability, sometimes even concealing them. An example would be quoting a political opponent against a public official anonymously, without identifying that significant characteristic of the source.

The habit of using unnamed sources on the naive— or cynical—assumption that, because something was said at all, it then was true, seriously weakens the credibility of many stories and many reporters.

The editor of *Newsweek*, Rick Smith, summarized the current criticism of the press in seeking to inspire the 1984 graduating class of his alma mater, Albion College, to help the media help itself:

> We [journalists] had proven ourselves to be the tenacious watchdogs of American society. But who was watching us? The searchlight . . . has uncovered our abuses . . . many Americans now express serious doubts about the techniques used to gather and report the news. Unidentified sources . . . ambush interviews . . . trial by allegation . . . instant analysis . . . impersonation . . . are all questionable, yet increasingly commonplace, ways to "get the story." As a result, the press has acquired a reputation for being sneaky, devious, and even untrustworthy.
>
> How has the press responded? Too often we have run for cover. We have hidden from our critics. And worst of all, we have hidden behind the First Amendment.

Tom Wicker adds a larger and more substantive complaint. He feels the media generally is too prone to promote what it believes is easiest for people to accept and in the process fails to cover significant issues adequately.

The criticism that is set out here easily could be offset with generous accolades from sources equally credible. That is not the point. No one is more eager than I to proclaim how successfully the press has done its job over the last couple of hundred years, or how much better government might do its job. Still, we must recognize the fact that this nation currently is debating—in the place where we make the rules, the Supreme Court—whether or not to limit the freedom of the press despite its good record of 200 years.

The possibility of limitation is a real one. I believe it requires that we admit the media's confessions of imperfection and what appears to be a disconcertingly serious loss of public favor that could encourage restrictions of First Amendment rights.

The first thing we must do is sound the alert and make it clear that we are facing a real threat of restriction of the constitutional freedom of the press. That is not easy. The drift of the Supreme Court does not get reported in the morning headlines. It is an elusive subject to which we must direct attention. Then, we must hope—and we cannot be sure it will work—that the reaction will affect, for the better, both the press and the courts.

In New York, we already have created a strong tradition of governmental support for freedom of both speech and the press. We have worked to give the press and the public the fullest possible opportunity to know and report on the workings of our state government. Freedom of information laws, open meetings laws, whistleblower laws, unique disclosure requirements, shield laws, and maximum accessibility for the benefit of the press on a day-to-day basis have been hallmarks of our administrations since 1975, and will continue to be as long as I am governor.

In the end, I think the best answer to the threat to the First Amendment is going to be found, as Fred Friendly, former president of CBS News, put it, "Not in the courtrooms but in the newsrooms of America."

One of the miracles of this democracy is that all of us— both the press and the public—are free to make the choices. We must work to keep it that way, to keep the miracle alive.

Mario M. Cuomo became a lawyer in 1956, and in 1963 he became a partner in the New York law firm of Corner, Cuomo, and Charles. He left the firm in 1975 to serve as secretary of state in New York. Four years later he became New York's lieutenant governor, and in 1983 he was elected governor of New York. Cuomo was reelected in 1986 and again in 1990.

Starting Time		Finishing Time	
Reading Time		Reading Rate	
Comprehension		Vocabulary	

Comprehension— Read the following questions and statements. For each one, put an *x* in the box before the option that contains the most complete or accurate answer. Check your answers in the Answer Key on page 106.

1. Franklin Delano Roosevelt created the Dunce Cap Club to
   - ☐ a. preserve the freedom of the press.
   - ☐ b. avoid exposure to the media.
   - ☐ c. chide members of the press.
   - ☐ d. honor reporters.

2. The Founding Fathers knew that the press was
   - ☐ a. nonpartisan.
   - ☐ b. imperfect.
   - ☐ c. weak.
   - ☐ d. well-intentioned.

3. The press played a large role in which of the following incidents?
   - ☐ a. the Triangle Waste Fire
   - ☐ b. the establishment of the Supreme Court
   - ☐ c. the Teapot Dome scandal
   - ☐ d. the founding of Albion College

4. Freedom of the press is a
   - ☐ a. worthy, but unattainable, goal.
   - ☐ b. necessity for all civilized nations.
   - ☐ c. principle worth fighting for.
   - ☐ d. concept that is uniquely American.

5. The press has a hard time
   - ☐ a. getting access to public officials.
   - ☐ b. capturing the attention of the public.
   - ☐ c. ferreting out the truth.
   - ☐ d. accepting criticism.

6. The press needs to
   - ☐ a. maintain high journalistic standards.
   - ☐ b. seek assistance from the federal government.
   - ☐ c. reassess its role as public watchdog.
   - ☐ d. return to the practices of 18th century journalism.

7. Politicians and members of the press have
   - ☐ a. different objectives.
   - ☐ b. nothing in common.
   - ☐ c. a finely tuned sense of morality.
   - ☐ d. betrayed the public.

8. The opening paragraph of the selection is written with
   - ☐ a. sarcasm.
   - ☐ b. pride.
   - ☐ c. animosity.
   - ☐ d. embarrassment.

9. The author believes the First Amendment to the Constitution has proven to be
   - ☐ a. a dangerous weapon.
   - ☐ b. a good thing.
   - ☐ c. ineffective.
   - ☐ d. helpful to politicians.

10. When the author states that changes in the law may "weaken the fabric of this society," he is using
    - ☐ a. literal language.
    - ☐ b. sound-words.
    - ☐ c. a metaphor.
    - ☐ d. a simile.

Comprehension Skills

1. recalling specific facts	6. making a judgment
2. retaining concepts	7. making an inference
3. organizing facts	8. recognizing tone
4. understanding the main idea	9. understanding characters
5. drawing a conclusion	10. appreciation of literary forms

Study Skills, Part One—Following is a passage with blanks where words have been omitted. Next to the passage are groups of five words, one group for each blank. Complete the passage by selecting the correct word for each of the blanks.

Recognizing Words, II

Even as a beginning reader, you cannot long escape some of the more complex problems of phonics. You must recognize short versus long ___(1)___ : *can* versus *cane.* You must learn the sounds produced by combinations of vowels: *round, fear, field, moon, rain.* You must learn that

(1)   stories   words
      vowels   thoughts   syllables

certain __(2)__ combinations produce their own sounds: *th*ing, *th*at, *ch*ance, *sh*ape, *ph*one. You must struggle with the peculiarities of the English language: *write, wright, right; through, enough; weather, whether.*

If you suspect that you are weak in phonics, seek the advice of your instructor or a __(3)__ specialist. There are materials available that can help strengthen your skills.

2. Sight Vocabulary. The more you read, the more good readers build their sight vocabularies—words that can be recognized at a glance without __(4)__ them out. In fact, it would be pure drudgery to read if every word had to be sounded out each time it was seen.

School children today are encouraged to learn lists of sight words. But some students have never mastered the basic sight words. This causes __(5)__ and loss of meaning of some of the easiest words. Anyone with this problem may not enjoy reading and may face real trouble in subjects with a heavy reading load.

Naturally, the more words you can __(6)__ on sight, the fewer you will have to sound out while you are reading.

Your reading, then, is a complex combination of physical, mechanical, and mental processes. Strengthening your reading requires an awareness of each process and __(7)__ where you are weak. Serious problems in any one area can cause serious reading difficulties that you should take steps to correct at once.

(2)	letter		vowel
	sentence	word	new

(3)	medical		reading
	mathematics	writing	material

(4)	printing		sounding
	reading	thinking	counting

(5)	embarrassment		racing
	stumbling	progress	improvement

(6)	learn		recognize
	discover	discard	reduce

(7)	repetition		patience
	practice	discipline	delay

Study Skills, Part Two—Read the study skills passage again, paying special attention to the lesson being taught. Then, without looking back at the passage, complete each sentence below by writing in the missing word or words. Check the Answer Key on page 106 for the answers to Study Skills, Part One, and Study Skills, Part Two.

1. The peculiarities of the English _____ present problems in the study of phonics.

2. Materials are available to strengthen your _____ .

3. Words recognized without sounding them out make up your _____ vocabulary.

4. Students who have not mastered basic sight words may not _____ reading.

5. Reading is a complex combination of physical, mechanical, and _____ processes.

5 | Lincoln's Last Day

by Stanley W. McClure

Vocabulary—The five words below are from the story you are about to read. Study the words and their meanings. Then complete the ten sentences that follow, using one of the five words to fill in the blank in each sentence. Mark your answer by writing the letter of the word on the line before the sentence. Check your answers in the Answer Key on page 106.

A. capitulation: surrender

B. anticipated: expected

C. scheme: system; plan

D. engaged: contracted for the use of; reserved

E. intent: concentrated; engrossed

_____ 1. Mr. Ashmun never had the meeting he _____ .

_____ 2. President Lincoln was happy and relieved about the _____ of Confederate forces.

_____ 3. The audience was _____ upon the play when President Lincoln arrived.

_____ 4. The doorkeeper at Ford's Theatre had no inkling of Booth's _____ .

_____ 5. Ford's Theatre routinely _____ people to act as stagehands.

_____ 6. Harry Hawk was _____ upon playing the part of Asa Trenchard when Booth approached the President's box.

_____ 7. No one in the audience _____ the assassination of President Lincoln that night.

_____ 8. The _____ of Lee meant the end of the Civil War.

_____ 9. Because Henry Rathbone rode to the theater with the President, he never _____ a carriage for that evening.

_____ 10. The overall _____ of the evening called for the Lincolns and their guests to occupy boxes 7 and 8.

April 14, 1865, was a day of celebration and thanksgiving in the Northern States. After four long years of war General Lee had surrendered, and the capitulation of Johnston's forces was expected soon. President Lincoln had chosen this day as a fitting occasion for again raising the shell-torn flag above Fort Sumter, on the fourth anniversary of its fall into Southern hands.

An hourly account of the events preceding the assassination

As a temporary escape from his arduous duties, Lincoln had arranged to attend the play at Ford's Theatre that evening. In the morning he breakfasted with his family; and Robert Lincoln, a captain on Grant's staff who had arrived the day before from City Point, Virginia, entertained them with accounts of life at the front. President Lincoln met with his Cabinet at 11 A.M., the session lasting until 1:30 P.M. The main topic of discussion was the restoration of the Southern States into the Union. During the afternoon the President took a long carriage ride with Mrs. Lincoln and Tad. The drive carried Lincoln to the Navy Yard where he visited the monitor *Montauk*. Returning to the White House, he spent a pleasant hour with Governor Oglesby and General Haynie, two of his old Illinois friends. After dinner Lincoln visited the War Department and then prepared to go to the theater. Several people were interviewed from 7:30 to 8 P.M., including Schuyler Colfax, Speaker of the House, who called by appointment. A congressman from Massachusetts, George Ashmun, called on the President regarding the claim of a client. It was after 8 o'clock and time to go to the theater. So that Ashmun would be admitted early the next morning, Lincoln wrote on a card "Allow Mr. Ashmun & friend to come in at 9 A.M. tomorrow. A. Lincoln. April 14, 1865." This was the last writing from the hand of Abraham Lincoln.

The Play: *Our American Cousin*

Tom Taylor's celebrated comedy, *Our American Cousin,* was presented at Ford's Theatre on the evening of April 14, 1865. The distinguished actress, Laura Keene, was in the role of Florence Trenchard, a character she had enacted more than 1,000 times. It was announced in the afternoon newspapers that General Grant would accompany President and Mrs. Lincoln to the theater. Although Lincoln was a familiar figure at Ford's Theatre, Grant was almost a total stranger, and Washingtonians were anxious for a glimpse of him. In the hope of seeing General Grant, many persons purchased tickets for the play, and a crowded house was anticipated.

A messenger from the Executive Mansion had come to the box office at Ford's Theatre at 10:30 on the morning of April 14th and reserved the state box for the Presidential party. Earlier in the morning, General and Mrs. Grant had accepted an invitation from the President to accompany him and Mrs. Lincoln to the theater.

Preparations for the Presidential Party

In preparation for the occasion the acting manager, Harry Clay Ford, supervised the decoration of the President's box, situated on the south side of the stage. The partition between the two upper boxes was removed by Edman Spangler, the stagehand, converting it into a single box for the convenience of the Presidential party. Two American flags, each on a staff, were placed at either side of the box and two others were draped on the balustrades. The blue regimental flag of the U.S. Treasury Guards was suspended at the center pillar on a staff. An engraving of George Washington was hung in front of the pillar as an added touch to the decorative scheme.

During the afternoon General Grant informed the President that he and Mrs. Grant would be unable to go to the theater. Late in the day they left by train for Philadelphia on the way to visit their children in Burlington, N.J. Lincoln then asked several other persons to join the theater party, but all, including Robert Lincoln, declined. At the last moment Miss Clara Harris, daughter of Senator Ira T. Harris of New York and her fiance, Major Henry R. Rathbone, accepted the invitation.

It was close to 8:15 P.M. when the Lincoln carriage left the White House grounds and drove toward the residence of Senator Harris, at 15th and H Streets NW. It was about 8:30 P.M. when the carriage drew up in front of Ford's Theatre. The performance had begun at 7:45 P.M. The house was filled, except for the boxes. Only the state box was reserved that evening.

There were five doorways opening into Ford's Theatre. The stairway leading to the family circle (gallery) was reached by the doorway on the extreme south. The next doorway on the north was the main entrance. The box office, with windows on the north and south, was located between these two doors. The other three doorways on the north were used as exits.

Entering the lobby of the theater by the main entrance, the Presidential party ascended the stairway at the north end to the dress circle. Charles Forbes, the footman, and John Parker, a special guard waiting at the theater, were in the party. Passing in back of the dress circle seats, they proceeded down the aisle to the vestibule leading to the double box.

The door to box 7, on the left side of the vestibule, was closed. The party entered through the open door to box 8, at the far end of the passage. In the afternoon, a sofa, a high-backed chair, and a black walnut rocking chair upholstered in red damask had been placed in the box.

The rockers of the rocking chair fitted into the angle of box 7, behind the closed door, and nearest to the audience.

The President took this chair with Mrs. Lincoln on his right, toward the center pillar of the double box. Miss Harris was seated on the right-hand corner of box 8 and Major Rathbone at her left on the sofa.

When the President entered the theater, William Withers, Jr., the leader of the orchestra, signaled for "Hail to the Chief." The audience then caught sight of the President and, rising as a body, cheered again and again. In acknowledgment, the President came to the front of the box and smilingly bowed to the audience. After the Presidential party was seated, the play was resumed.

Events Preceding the Assassination

At noon Booth walked to Ford's Theatre, where it was his custom to have his mail delivered. Several letters were handed to him, and he seated himself on the doorsill to read them. After half an hour Booth walked on. He was told by Harry Ford that the President and General Grant would be at the theater that evening.

Booth then went to the livery stable of James W. Pumphrey, on C Street in the rear of the National Hotel, and engaged a small bay mare which he called for about 4 o'clock. Sometime later he put the horse in his stable in the rear of Ford's Theatre. Edman Spangler, the stagehand, and Joseph "Peanuts" Burroughs, who distributed bills and was stage doorkeeper at Ford's Theatre, were in charge of the stable.

Shortly after 9 o'clock, Booth came to the back door of the theater and called for Spangler to hold his horse. Spangler was one of the sceneshifters and his almost continuous presence was required at his post. As soon as Booth passed inside, Spangler called for "Peanuts" Burroughs to watch the horse.

Booth crossed underneath the stage to an exit leading to 10th Street and entered the saloon of Peter Taltavull, adjoining the theater on the south. Instead of his customary brandy, Booth ordered whiskey and a glass of water.

Booth walked out and entered the theater lobby. He was in and out of the lobby several times and once asked the time of the doorkeeper, John Buckingham. A short time later, at 10:10 P.M., he reentered the lobby, ascended the stairs, and passed around the dress circle to the vestibule door leading to the President's box. Before reaching the door, Booth paused, took off his hat, leaned against the wall, and made a survey of the audience and stage. The play was now nearing the close of the second scene of Act 3. According to witnesses, Booth took a card from his pocket and handed it to Charles Forbes who occupied seat 300, the one nearest the vestibule door. He then stepped down one step, put his hand on the door of the corridor, and placed his knee against it. It opened and Booth entered, closing it behind him.

As it had no lock, Booth placed a pine bar against the door and anchored the other end in a mortise cut into the outside brick wall of the building. This precaution was taken to prevent anyone in the dress circle from following. A small hole which had been bored in the door of box 7, directly in back of Lincoln, enabled the assassin to view the position of the President. The actor had free access to the theater at all times. It is probable that the mortise in the wall was cut by Booth sometime after the rehearsal on April 14. Notwithstanding the general belief that Booth also bored the hole in the door to the President's box, Frank Ford, the son of Harry Clay Ford, later said that his father had the hole cut so the guard could look in on the Presidential party without having to open the door.

The actor timed his entrance into the box when only one person was on the stage. The lone figure of Harry Hawk, playing the part of Asa Trenchard, was standing at the center of the stage in front of the curtained doorway at the tragic moment. Miss Clara Harris and Major Rathbone were intent upon the play and Mrs. Lincoln laughed at the words being spoken by Harry Hawk: "Don't know the manners of good society, eh? Well, I guess I know enough to turn you inside out, old gal—you sockdologizing old mantrap." These words were probably the last heard by Abraham Lincoln.

Starting Time		Finishing Time	
Reading Time		Reading Rate	
Comprehension		Vocabulary	

Comprehension — Read the following questions and statements. For each one, put an *x* in the box before the option that contains the most complete or accurate answer. Check your answers in the Answer Key on page 106.

1. The last note that Lincoln wrote concerned
   □ a. Harry Hawk.
   □ b. Schuyler Colfax.
   □ c. George Ashmun.
   □ d. Henry Rathbone.

2. President Lincoln's reception at the theater was
   □ a. enthusiastic.
   □ b. unexpected.
   □ c. guarded.
   □ d. resented.

3. Before going into the theater that evening, Booth
  □ a. blocked the vestibule door.
  □ b. bribed the guard.
  □ c. handed a note to Charles Forbes.
  □ d. drank some whiskey.

4. This selection sheds light on
  □ a. a little-known event.
  □ b. an evil conspiracy.
  □ c. a national tragedy.
  □ d. one man's insanity.

5. Security at the theater was
  □ a. extreme.
  □ b. unnecessary.
  □ c. normal.
  □ d. poor.

6. Lincoln's last day was
  □ a. marked by political confusion.
  □ b. normal in every way.
  □ c. ruined by family tensions.
  □ d. spent in guarded isolation.

7. Evidence seems to suggest that Booth
  □ a. was suffering from a serious mental disorder.
  □ b. had made plans to escape by horse.
  □ c. was part of a general conspiracy.
  □ d. had no advance knowledge of Lincoln's plans.

8. The tone of the selection is
  □ a. emotional.
  □ b. threatening.
  □ c. theatrical.
  □ d. factual.

9. Booth was a
  □ a. confused man.
  □ b. serene man.
  □ c. calculating man.
  □ d. forgiving man.

10. The facts of the selection seem
  □ a. sketchy.
  □ b. poorly researched.
  □ c. well documented.
  □ d. disorganized.

Comprehension Skills

1. recalling specific facts	6. making a judgment
2. retaining concepts	7. making an inference
3. organizing facts	8. recognizing tone
4. understanding the main idea	9. understanding characters
5. drawing a conclusion	10. appreciation of literary forms

Study Skills, Part One—Following is a passage with blanks where words have been omitted. Next to the passage are groups of five words, one group for each blank. Complete the passage by selecting the correct word for each of the blanks.

Patterns of Thought

Authors use different patterns of thought in developing their paragraphs. The reader who understands these patterns has the key to ___(1)___ reading—the art of extracting the topic sentence or key statement from each paragraph.

You recall from your English classes that a paragraph is defined as a group of ___(2)___ developing one idea. Authors use certain methods of developing this idea, and these methods can be classified into identifiable patterns. Recognizing the pattern permits the reader to find the main idea quickly and see how it has been developed. Students who have difficulty distinguishing between main ideas and subordinate details will find the use of paragraph patterns of immense value.

SELECTIVE READING

We have been told of the late President John Kennedy's ability to read at speeds of 1,200 words-per-minute, picking out the ___(3)___ ideas. This kind of reading is called selective reading.

(1)
  interesting   educational
  basic   selective   rapid

(2)
  words   sentences
  adjectives   phrases   thoughts

(3)
  key   complete
  total   unimportant   insignificant

Selective reading techniques are additional skills needed by the ___(4)___ reader. Good reading is really many different kinds of reading, each suitable for a particular reading occasion.

The skills of using patterns of paragraph development are part of the selective reading ___(5)___ needed to become a flexible reader. We will discuss the eleven popular ___(6)___ employed by authors to present and develop their main ideas. The student who can master the techniques of ___(7)___ and using patterns of thought will have at his disposal the ability to pick out the key ideas in any material he is reading.

Plan now to study and learn the paragraph patterns which will be discussed in this text.

(4)   intelligent   active
    interested   enthusiastic   flexible

(5)   ideas   thoughts
    examples   techniques   paragraphs

(6)   patterns   selections
    parts   styles   descriptions

(7)   organizing   memorizing
    recognizing   selecting   reading

Study Skills, Part Two—Read the study skills passage again, paying special attention to the lesson being taught. Then, without looking back at the passage, complete each sentence below by writing in the missing word or words. Check the Answer Key on page 106 for the answers to Study Skills, Part One, and Study Skills, Part Two.

1. Authors use different patterns of _____ in developing their paragraphs.

2. Recognizing the pattern permits the reader to find the _____ quickly and see how it has been developed.

3. Students who have difficulty distinguishing between main ideas and _____ will find the use of paragraph patterns of immense value.

4. Selective reading means picking out key _____ .

5. Selective reading techniques are additional _____ needed by the flexible reader.

6 | Winning the Battle of the Bug, I

by William Shelton

Vocabulary—The five words below are from the story you are about to read. Study the words and their meanings. Then complete the ten sentences that follow, using one of the five words to fill in the blank in each sentence. Mark your answer by writing the letter of the word on the line before the sentence. Check your answers in the Answer Key on page 106.

A. rancid: rotten; putrid

B. pestilence: deadly epidemic disease

C. contaminates: infects; taints

D. formidable: arousing fear or dread

E. ominous: threatening; menacing

_____ 1. _____ prevented the French from completing a canal across Panama.

_____ 2. Despite its size, the mosquito has long been a _____ enemy of man.

_____ 3. Tests show that the pesticide DDT _____ many living things.

_____ 4. Mosquitoes are repelled by certain _____ odors.

_____ 5. Some experts worry that mosquitoes will spread a new _____ across the land.

_____ 6. In 1933 the _____ spread of St. Louis encephalitis had many people worried.

_____ 7. Jet travel may present a _____ new obstacle to control of mosquito-transmitted diseases.

_____ 8. Biologists worry about using a pesticide that _____ man's environment.

_____ 9. The knowledge that mosquitoes carry 150 different diseases makes their familiar buzz seem all the more _____ .

_____ 10. _____ grease was once used as a mosquito repellent.

They surpass in population and total weight all the other animals on the earth combined.

The confrontation begins when a small, fragile insect lights gently on your hand. It thrusts a hollow probe through the tender cells of your skin and into a vessel where your blood courses. You feel a slight sting. Because you are hurt, you react instinctively. A mosquito! Swat it!

If you are quick and your attacker is slow, you demolish this most ancient of enemies. But who really won? The million-year-old man? Or the 50-million-year-old mosquito? Perhaps you've won the battle, but the mosquito may win the war. For among the 150 diseases which the mosquito is known to carry are yellow fever and malaria which together have accounted for one-half of all human deaths in history.

In order to dine, the mosquito first injects a saliva-like liquid into your flesh which keeps your blood from coagulating as she sucks it out. (Only the females bite.) In that saliva medical science has identified the causes of such worldwide plagues as dengue fever, filariasis (which results in elephantiasis), and epidemic hemorrhagic fever, which in one five-month period in South Vietnam caused 116 deaths. In the United States alone, scientists have found five types of human encephalitis viruses, including the dreaded Western and St. Louis encephalitis which causes swelling of human brain tissues. The Venezuelan variety (VEE) usually causes only influenza-like symptoms in man, but in the summer of 1971, VEE killed over half of the horses it infected in the Southwest.

Like the tiny Lilliputians that subdued Gulliver, the "skeeter" acquires strength through sheer numbers. There are several hundred varieties of *Culicidae* in the United States, and over 2,000 worldwide. They surpass in population and total weight all the other animals of the earth combined. And mosquitoes breed equally as well in polar region ice pools, tree holes in tropical rain forests, or in the numerous receptacles of technological man—from tin cans to cemetery urns.

"The mosquito, except for man himself," says scientist Gilbert Chambers who researched the mosquito problem at the request of Exxon Oil & Refining Company, "is the cleverest, most destructive, and most adaptable animal on the face of the earth today. Man has always fought the mosquito, but has only experienced a measure of success in the last 60 years or so."

If he had nothing with which to defend himself but his swat, man would have little chance against the mosquito. Early man smeared rancid grease on his body as a mosquito repellent, or hid within a cloud of woodsmoke from his campfire. The ingenious Egyptians improved on the campfire by developing the smudge pot and learning to weave mosquito netting. Hordes of mosquitoes from the Pontine Marshes surrounding ancient

Rome so plagued the Caesars that they began what may have been man's first organized effort to fight back on a large scale. They drained the marshes, a mosquito control project which took fourteen centuries to complete.

The mosquito is partly responsible for the fact that the official language of the United States is neither Spanish nor French. Yellow fever and malaria contained early Spanish expansion in the New World, and turned back Napoleon's expeditionary forces in the Caribbean in 1802. Late in the nineteenth century, the same pestilence halted French attempts to dig a canal across the Isthmus of Panama.

Mosquito-borne diseases prevented mankind from expanding into the lush tropic zones of the earth, with the result that (with the exception of the polar regions) the vast equatorial lands are still the least populated of the world. Colonists settling the eastern shores of North America suffered from malaria, and some authorities believe it was the *Anopheles* mosquito which forced the English to move their capital from Jamestown to Williamsburg in 1699.

Until recently, few methods existed for controlling mosquito infestations. As early as 1793, Philadelphians poured expensive whale oil onto the surface of water in rain barrels to prevent mosquitoes from breeding there. With the birth of the oil industry, kerosene came into experimental use as a mosquito control during the 1890s. A major breakthrough came around the turn of the century when Dr. Walter Reed identified the female *Aedes aegypti* mosquito as the carrier of yellow fever. With this information, the United States took over the job of digging the Panama Canal. A massive program of swamp drainage and spraying with kerosene brought mosquitoes under control sufficiently to permit completion of the Canal in 1914.

In the early part of this century, mosquitoes got so bad in New Jersey that farmers were unable to farm and industry around Newark had to shut down temporarily on several occasions. To combat the "New Jersey Terror," the state established the first U.S. mosquito control program. They sprayed millions of gallons of undiluted diesel oil on the waters of coastal marshes in amounts of 20 gallons or more an acre. The oil damaged aquatic and plant life, but it killed mosquitoes and brought the Terror under control. Encouraged by these results, other states, including Florida, adopted similar programs. Today, there are some 350 organized mosquito control districts active in the U.S. Altogether, they spend some $50 million a year to kill mosquitoes.

But the mosquito has continued to fight back. In 1922 two million people caught dengue fever in Gulf Coast states. In 1933 mosquitoes killed 200 Missourians by infecting them with St. Louis encephalitis.

Then, in the 1940s, the world was handed a new weapon so miraculously effective against mosquitoes that some authorities boldly predicted victory in man's battle with the bug. The wonder-weapon was DDT. Dusted, sprayed, or fogged, DDT meant death to both adult and larval mosquitoes. Used throughout the world during the following decades, the chemical saved millions of people from disease and prevented countless deaths. Unfortunately, man has learned that his wonder-weapon has disadvantages. It isn't selective; it kills or contaminates creatures other than mosquitoes. It isn't readily biodegradable, and can be passed along the food chain in increasingly concentrated quantity from tiny organisms that ingest it to larger species that ingest them and eventually to man. And, finally, a few mosquitoes strong enough to survive the nerve-paralyzing effects of DDT have produced offspring capable of resisting the poison. Today, DDT is largely ineffective as a mosquito control agent in most of the United States.

As these problems came to be recognized in the mosquito control districts of the country, entomologists turned to new organophosphate pesticides as an alternative to DDT. Introduced during the 1950s, these poisons proved effective for a time. Before long, however, mosquitoes in some areas developed immunity to organophosphates as well as DDT. The formidable combination of vast numbers and rapid life cycle is capable of producing pesticide-resistant generations faster than science can concoct new poisons. And man seems to be running out of poisons to try.

Two ominous news reports recently highlighted the problem. A story in *The New York Times* reported, "Two species of mosquitoes native to California have acquired complete immunity to all man-made pesticides." A month later the first paragraph of a widely published Associated Press dispatch read, "A type of mosquito which can infect humans with deadly sleeping sickness is reported out of control in California because it has developed immunity to all known pesticides."

A biologist specializing in mosquito control, whose experience includes both the Central Valley and the Rio Grande Valley in Texas, looks at the problem this way: "I don't want to be identified as a doomsday man," he says, "but the situation could get out of hand." With jet travel now commonplace, he suggests the possibility that poison-resistant mosquitoes could carry a fatal disease from one country to another without warning. "I live in fear that some Asian virus might mutate to a fatal disease—as the dengue fever virus did—and come sweeping out of there so fast that we couldn't stop it," he says.

Starting Time		*Finishing Time*	
Reading Time		*Reading Rate*	
Comprehension		*Vocabulary*	

Comprehension — Read the following questions and statements. For each one, put an *x* in the box before the option that contains the most complete or accurate answer. Check your answers in the Answer Key on page 106.

1. DDT does not
   - ☐ a. affect large animals.
   - ☐ b. pose any danger to man.
   - ☐ c. decompose quickly.
   - ☐ d. spare any mosquitoes.

2. The mosquito is
   - ☐ a. surprisingly vulnerable.
   - ☐ b. obviously predictable.
   - ☐ c. extraordinarily adaptable.
   - ☐ d. unfortunately misunderstood.

3. Ways were found to rid large areas of mosquitoes, but not without
   - ☐ a. unnecessary loss of life.
   - ☐ b. unreasonable public opposition.
   - ☐ c. damage to the environment.
   - ☐ d. serious loss of jobs.

4. Science is faced with the problem of developing poisons which will destroy mosquitoes
   - ☐ a. without costing too much.
   - ☐ b. in heavily populated areas.
   - ☐ c. which infect domesticated animals.
   - ☐ d. without destroying mankind.

5. Experience with DDT and organophosphate pesticides illustrates the
   - ☐ a. helplessness of science.
   - ☐ b. incompetence of scientists.
   - ☐ c. vulnerablility of mosquitoes.
   - ☐ d. hardiness of the mosquito.

6. The concern expressed by the biologist specializing in mosquito control is
   - ☐ a. realistic.
   - ☐ b. exaggerated.
   - ☐ c. groundless.
   - ☐ d. amusing.

7. The dreaded mosquito has
   ☐ a. halted the advance of civilization.
   ☐ b. influenced the course of history.
   ☐ c. united the nations of the world.
   ☐ d. proven no match for modern technology.

8. The selection sounds a note of
   ☐ a. terror.   ☐ c. alarm.
   ☐ b. optimism.   ☐ d. indignation.

9. The mosquito's resilience has left mosquito-control experts
   ☐ a. relieved.   ☐ c. exasperated.
   ☐ b. disoriented.   ☐ d. outraged.

10. The selection could be classified as
    ☐ a. a debate.
    ☐ b. a report.
    ☐ c. an essay.
    ☐ d. a short story.

Study Skills, Part One—Following is a passage with blanks where words have been omitted. Next to the passage are groups of five words, one group for each blank. Complete the passage by selecting the correct word for each of the blanks.

The Fable Paragraph

The first pattern of ___(1)___ development that we are going to examine is called the Fable. This pattern begins with a story or illustration and then presents the conclusion, moral, or generalization drawn from that illustration. In this sense it is like a fable: a story comes first to ___(2)___ the moral presented at the end.

___(3)___ the Fable paragraph looks like this:

STORY

OR

ILLUSTRATION

MAIN IDEA

Here is an example of the Fable:

   In my student days, I once knew a professor, an eminent psychologist, who was a little daft on the subject of the Roosevelt ___(4)___ . Every act of the president, every program proposed, every law enacted was interpreted by him as a bid for more power, an example of creeping socialism, a collaboration with communists. You need not be ___(5)___ to New Deal policies or practices to understand why I sat rapt when he spoke on psychology and only psychology.

   Once the reader ___(6)___ a Fable paragraph, he knows where to find the main idea. This is the author's point—

(1)   story   character
   vocabulary   sentence   paragraph

(2)   illustrate   demonstrate
   describe   compare   discuss

(3)   Typically   Graphically
   Ideally   Usually   Occasionally

(4)   cabinet   administration
   admiration   determination   relaxation

(5)   congenial   resistant
   sympathetic   hostile   opposed

(6)   overlooks   denies
   completes   recognizes   rejects

that is what he wants the reader to understand and learn. The story illustrating this point may be interesting but it is not __(7)__ in itself. It is not to be memorized or remembered.

(7)   relevant   important
      insignificant   trivial   helpful

Study Skills, Part Two—Read the study skills passage again, paying special attention to the lesson being taught. Then, without looking back at the passage, complete each sentence below by writing in the missing word or words. Check the Answer Key on page 106 for the answers to Study Skills, Part One, and Study Skills, Part Two.

1. The Fable paragraph begins with a _____ .

2. It ends with a conclusion, _____ , or generalization.

3. In the example given, the writer was relieved when the professor spoke about _____ and not about the Roosevelt administration.

4. The reader knows that the main idea in the Fable paragraph is usually at the _____ of the paragraph.

5. As long as the student understands the main idea, it is not necessary to remember the _____ .

7 | Winning the Battle of the Bug, II

by William Shelton

Vocabulary—The five words below are from the story you are about to read. Study the words and their meanings. Then complete the ten sentences that follow, using one of the five words to fill in the blank in each sentence. Mark your answer by writing the letter of the word on the line before the sentence. Check your answers in the Answer Key on page 107.

A. enhanced: increased

B. derive: obtain; extract

C. enumerated: listed

D. vulnerable: susceptible to attack

E. lethal: deadly

_____ 1. Flit MLO has _____ the prospects of bringing the mosquito population under control.

_____ 2. Even small doses of 3855-2 have proven _____ to mosquito larvae.

_____ 3. Mosquito larvae are more _____ to Flit MLO than they are to DDT.

_____ 4. Mosquito larvae _____ their oxygen from the air.

_____ 5. No one has _____ any reasons why 3855-2 should not be used.

_____ 6. Flit MLO is not _____ to humans.

_____ 7. People can _____ hope from the success of 3855-2.

_____ 8. Mosquito larvae are _____ to anything which interferes with their ability to take in oxygen.

_____ 9. Scientists have _____ several reasons why 3855-2 is superior to DDT.

_____ 10. The work of Chambers and Micks has not _____ man's ability to kill adult mosquitoes.

Victory may be near through a new and powerful weapon.

All is not yet lost. Man's chances of victory over the mosquito have been enhanced by a new and powerful weapon developed during eight years of team effort on the part of Exxon Research and Engineering Company and The University of Texas Medical Branch at Galveston. The weapon is a clear, almost odorless liquid which bears the laboratory research designation 3855-2.

Demonstrating 3855-2, Nina Gaddy, a technician in the Galveston lab of Dr. Don Micks, chairman of the University's Department of Preventive Medicine and Community Health, places 25 mosquito larvae in a beaker of water. Using a microsyringe, she drips just .005 milliliters (a tiny fraction of a drop) into the beaker. The liquid instantly spreads over the water's surface.

Although mosquito larvae live in water, they derive oxygen from the air. From time to time, they must come to the surface like snorkelers to breathe. Soon, the first wriggler rises to the top. At the surface, it opens the trap-door of its siphon tube and inhales a snootful of trouble. Instantly, it bends and twists, biting its tail where the siphon tube is located. For several minutes, it "doughnuts" frantically, using up its oxygen. Again and again, it tries to breathe but takes in more of the thin liquid floating on the water's surface. Soon it is joined in its death throes by other wrigglers stricken by the larvicide.

"In 48 hours, all 25 will be dead," Ms. Gaddy explains, "and after 72 hours, all of the larvicide will have disappeared."

Similar experiments have been performed thousands of times during a decade of searching for a better way to control mosquitoes. The search began with Gilbert Chambers, a chemist with special interests in wildlife management and water pollution. During the 1950s Chambers studied the effects of changes in water quality on the aquatic life in Texas coastal rivers and bays. As mosquitoes were part of this ecology, Chambers noted with interest the developing problem of poison immunity in insects. He wondered if there were some type of hydrocarbon which might be used as an effective substitute for poisons.

Sharing their extensive knowledge of the mosquito's life cycle, Chambers and Micks concluded that mosquitoes might be attacked most effectively at their weakest link, the water phase, when they are in their larval stage. Working in close collaboration, the team enumerated three specifications for the ideal mosquito control agent: It would kill larvae before they could emerge as adult mosquitoes. It would be harmless to other life and to humans. And it would frustrate the mosquito's ability to build up resistance and immunity. They decided upon a new approach to finding such a chemical. In past practice, researchers would normally select a chemical thought to have potential as a pesticide and then test it to see what types of pests it would kill. Chambers and Micks proposed to select mosquito larvae as a specific target, and then build a chemical out of hydrogen and carbon molecules which would meet the specifications for the ideal mosquito control agent.

Being close to Exxon's giant Baytown, Texas, refinery, Chambers was ideally set up to explore among the petroleum hydrocarbons for interesting compounds. As each substance was isolated, it was given a code number (to avoid all possible bias) and handed over to Dr. Micks who would then test it for effectiveness on mosquito larvae. Guided by Dr. Micks's reports, Chambers began altering the chemistry of the more successful compounds by adding, subtracting, or lengthening the component molecules. In time, the chemistry became so complex he had to use computers to work out variations. "We tested over 800 substances," Chambers recalls.

As they dug into the problem, the members of the industry-university team explored some little known areas of biology. The scientists tested different species of mosquitoes to see whether one would react differently to treatment by a hydrocarbon as compared to another. They checked response to hydrocarbons at various stages of a mosquito's growth to see whether it was more vulnerable early or late in its development. They sought answers to the question of whether the larvicide would readily enter the insect's respiratory system. They examined bits of tissue to see what kind of change or damage might have been caused. Bit by bit, the team assembled facts and found answers to their questions.

By the mid-'60s, several good mosquito killers had been isolated, but the one known as 3855-2 began to emerge from lab and field trials as the best. Even at rates of application far in excess of recommended levels, 3855-2 proved safe to fish, shrimp, and other crustaceans. It did affect some insects that spend a portion of their lives at the water's surface. But vegetation and small creatures such as bees, dogs, cats, rabbits, and birds weren't bothered by it. It was safe for people to handle. And it was lethal to mosquito larvae.

Dr. Micks explains that the substance kills mosquito larvae by interfering with their respiration. "Like man, mosquito larvae take oxygen directly into their cells. When this process is interfered with, the most damaging effect is hypoxia, or too little oxygen," he says. In addition, the studies show a type of irreversible cell damage that indicates more is at work than the "rope around the neck" principle.

Because the process, like the swat, is basically mechanical, there's little likelihood that mosquitoes can develop immunity or resistance. In lab tests to check this possibility, technicians reduced the dosage level until only half of a batch of mosquito larvae were killed. The survivors were allowed to breed, and their larvae put through the test. After 70 generations had been exposed, scientists could still find no evidence of developing immunity.

In 1966, mosquito control districts in Mississippi, Texas, and Louisiana conducted extensive field tests using the new larvicide. They found it as effective as lab tests suggested it would be. They also discovered one additional advantage not noticed in the lab. The development of larvae which failed to get a fatal dose of the larvicide was delayed for as much as nine days. This meant that larvae which must emerge quickly from such temporary habitats as pasture water would not survive.

In 1967, after 3855-2 passed all field evaluations, Exxon decided to place the product on the market, but with sales limited to mosquito control districts and public health agencies. Richard Slover, Marketing Specialist on Agricultural and Public Health Products, says Exxon decided to name the new larvicide Flit MLO after a household mosquito spray made famous in the 1930s by the advertising slogan, "Quick, Henry, the Flit!" Chemically and functionally, however, Flit MLO has no relationship to the original Flit, Slover says.

Introduced publicly at the International Congress of Tropical Medicine held in 1967 in Iran, Flit MLO was welcomed by mosquito control professionals. Using Exxon's minimum recommended dosage of one gallon of Flit MLO per acre of water, mosquito control districts can keep cost of treatment to about fifty cents an acre. They find they can apply it easily with simple spraying equipment.

In 1968, *Conservation News* and the National Wildlife Federation approved the new product because it is "not a chemical poison, therefore it's harmless to fish, wildlife, and vegetation. Mosquitoes cannot develop strains resistant to it, as they have to DDT." Nowhere in the districts and countries using Flit MLO has the resistance phenomenon been observed. Chambers and Dr. Micks do not believe it will ever occur.

Among others recommending Flit MLO is New York medical entomologist Dr. Thomas F. Bast. He prefers a three-pronged approach: Use of pesticides to get at the mosquito in its larva or pupa stage; biological controls, such as placing larvae-eating minnows in streams and ponds; and water management, including such methods as draining ditches and eliminating mosquito breeding places. He thinks such measures as fogging are not of much value. "It might look impressive, but it's very expensive and not very effective," he says. "It's not really mosquito control as much as it is people control. It's a great way to keep complaints down."

In time, "people control" may become unnecessary as mosquito control becomes a reality. In mosquito control districts throughout the United States, Henry and his counterparts are quickly fetching the Flit MLO. Meanwhile, back in Texas, the quiet search goes on as a productive alliance of industry and academe seeks to enlarge upon this breakthrough in the ongoing battle with the bug.

Starting Time		Finishing Time	
Reading Time		Reading Rate	
Comprehension		Vocabulary	

Comprehension— Read the following questions and statements. For each one, put an *x* in the box before the option that contains the most complete or accurate answer. Check your answers in the Answer Key on page 107.

1. To survive and prosper, mosquito larvae require
   - ☐ a. larvicide.
   - ☐ b. care and protection.
   - ☐ c. water and oxygen.
   - ☐ d. hydrocarbon.

2. Larvicide 3855-2 seems to be
   - ☐ a. an environmentalist's dream.
   - ☐ b. the only possible solution to the mosquito problem.
   - ☐ c. a potential threat to agriculture.
   - ☐ d. the answer to biological warfare.

3. Which of the following is not a specification for the ideal mosquito control agent?
   - ☐ a. Larvae must be killed at an early stage of development.
   - ☐ b. The control agent must kill the larvae quickly and effectively.
   - ☐ c. The control agent must be harmless to all other forms of life.
   - ☐ d. The mosquito must be unable to build up resistance and immunity.

4. The selection illustrates the
   - ☐ a. confusion which surrounds scientific investigations.
   - ☐ b. practical value of academic and industrial cooperation.
   - ☐ c. unrealistic long-term goals of science and industry.
   - ☐ d. losing battle being waged against the mosquito population.

5. The research technique used by Chambers and Micks was
   - ☐ a. a reversal of traditional techniques.
   - ☐ b. modeled after known techniques.
   - ☐ c. a daring departure from safe techniques.
   - ☐ d. encouraged by other scientists.

6. The liquid 3855-2 seems to be
   - ☐ a. unnecessarily destructive.
   - ☐ b. exorbitantly expensive.
   - ☐ c. unusually effective.
   - ☐ d. potentially dangerous.

7. The scientific method of investigation used by Chambers and Micks required
   - ☐ a. numerous safety precautions.
   - ☐ b. extensive federal funding.
   - ☐ c. special environmental controls.
   - ☐ d. elaborate record-keeping.

8. The general tone of the selection is
   - ☐ a. discouraging.
   - ☐ b. disturbing.
   - ☐ c. argumentative.
   - ☐ d. optimistic.

9. Chambers and Micks are both
   - ☐ a. arrogant perfectionists.
   - ☐ b. unpredictable eccentrics.
   - ☐ c. dedicated professionals.
   - ☐ d. reclusive scientists.

10. Chambers's comment that "We tested over 800 substances" is an example of
   - ☐ a. overstatement.
   - ☐ b. personification.
   - ☐ c. symbolism.
   - ☐ d. literal language.

Study Skills, Part One—Following is a passage with blanks where words have been omitted. Next to the passage are groups of five words, one group for each blank. Complete the passage by selecting the correct word for each of the blanks.

The Salestalk Paragraph

The next pattern of paragraph development we wish to consider is called the Salestalk. This pattern presents facts and details and closes with a generalization. Like a good ___(1)___ , this pattern gives the arguments first and then makes the ___(2)___ .

Graphically the Salestalk looks like this:

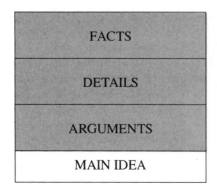

| FACTS |
| DETAILS |
| ARGUMENTS |
| MAIN IDEA |

(1)   teacher   carpenter
   politician   salesperson   architect

(2)   catch   pitch
   retreat   advance   throw

Here is an example of the Salestalk:

Finally, strive constantly to judge the ___(3)___ and value of the ideas you encounter in your reading. Do not act like a ___(4)___ , passively sopping up whatever the author has to offer. Maintain at all times a critical attitude. Criticism, after all, is only "the act or art of judging by some ___(5)___ ." When you weigh, you judge pro and con evidence of an issue. In other words, you think—and that is why you come to college: to learn how to think effectively.

This pattern is used a great deal in textbook paragraphs of ___(6)___ . The author will give details and facts and then present to the reader the main idea based on those facts.

Your job as a reader is to recognize the pattern and locate the main idea. With this in mind, you can read the facts and details, ___(7)___ understanding how they relate to the whole and to each other.

(3)   essence   meaning
     effort   source   truth

(4)   blotter   mirror
     robot   fighter   trainer

(5)   author   lesson
     standard   story   quality

(6)   introduction   information
     transition   illustration   application

(7)   knowingly   optimistically
     critically   carefully   negatively

Study Skills, Part Two—Read the study skills passage again, paying special attention to the lesson being taught. Then, without looking back at the passage, complete each sentence below by writing in the missing word or words. Check the Answer Key on page 107 for the answers to Study Skills, Part One, and Study Skills, Part Two.

1. The Salestalk paragraph presents facts and _____ at the beginning.

2. The end of this kind of paragraph contains the _____ .

3. The main idea of the sample paragraph is that students go to college to learn how to _____ effectively.

4. In order to achieve that goal, the student has to _____ the evidence of an issue.

5. The reader must understand how the facts given _____ to the whole and to each other.

8 | **Death with Dignity**

by Dr. Elizabeth Kubler-Ross

Vocabulary—The five words below are from the story you are about to read. Study the words and their meanings. Then complete the ten sentences that follow, using one of the five words to fill in the blank in each sentence. Mark your answer by writing the letter of the word on the line before the sentence. Check your answers in the Answer Key on page 107.

A. terminally ill: dying

B. fantasies: fanciful thoughts; daydreams

C. impending: about to take place; approaching

D. mortality: the unavoidability of death

E. facilitate: make easier

_____ 1. People who are _____ must grapple with many issues.

_____ 2. Homemaker services and shopping services would _____ home care for old people.

_____ 3. Children are usually isolated from any _____ deaths in their family.

_____ 4. Most people have _____ of living forever.

_____ 5. Many _____ people are left to die in institutions.

_____ 6. It is sometimes painful to think of our own _____ .

_____ 7. Traditional medical professionals pay little attention to the hopes and _____ of their dying patients.

_____ 8. Many people must face their _____ death alone, isolated from the ones they love.

_____ 9. Human _____ means that some day each of us will face death.

_____ 10. Talking with patients about death can _____ their acceptance of the inevitable.

I do not like to talk about dying with dignity, but I would like to talk about living with dignity, and I think that makes a difference.

I have interviewed over 500 terminally ill patients and asked them to share with us what it is like to be dying, what kinds of needs, fears, and fantasies those patients have, and, perhaps most important, to tell us what kind of things we can do, by which I mean family members and members of the helping professions, to be more helpful.

We started this project not as a research project or anything planned, but as a chance happening. I think it became important that I was born and raised in Switzerland. In the old country—and I guess in the old times in this country, also—death was part of life, like birth is.

When I was a child, people used to be born at home and often died at home. Dying patients were not very often institutionalized. This did not make dying easier for the dying patient, but I think most important of all, it helped the children and grandchildren to learn that death is part of life.

When I came to this country, I was very impressed that the children are not allowed to visit patients in hospitals or the mental institutions. Very seldom you hear the laughter of children in nursing homes. And I have seen hundreds of people in this country who have never experienced a death in the family. What we have learned from interviewing over 500 dying patients—and I am not talking about dying children, who, by the way, die much easier than grownups—the majority of our patients want very much to die at home. Yet, close to 80 percent of all patients interviewed died in an institution. Patients who can prepare themselves early and in a familiar, comfortable environment for their impending death are better able to finish their unfinished business, to put their house in order, as they pass through the stages of dying, as I have outlined in my book, *On Death and Dying.*

Family members still now believe that it is better "not to tell" the patient. We found the opposite to be true. If we will listen to the patient and talk with them about their illness, they will proceed much quicker to the stage of acceptance, and not resignation. Eighty percent of our patients in nursing homes want to die very much, but they are not in the stage of acceptance. They are in a stage of resignation, which is kind of a feeling of defeat, "what's the use; I am tired of living."

Need of the Patient for Hope

Patients have two basic essential needs when they are informed that they have a potentially fatal illness: The biggest need is always allow for hope. Hope is not the same

A transcript of Dr. Kubler-Ross's statement before the U.S. Senate Committee on Aging

as hope for cure treatment or prolongation of life. When a patient is dying, this hope will change to something that is not associated with cure treatment or prolongation of life.

To give you a practical example of how hope changes, like hope from the living to the hope of the dying, I visited a young mother with small children who had cancer. Each time I saw her, she said, "I hope those research laboratories work hard and I can get one of their new miracle drugs, and I get well." Naturally, I shared those hopes with her, though the probability was extremely slim.

One day I visited her, and she looked very different. She said, "Dr. Ross, a miracle happened." I said, "Did you get the new drugs?" She said, "No, I know now that these miracle drugs are not forthcoming, and I am no longer afraid." I asked her, "What is your hope now?" She said, "I hope my children are going to make it."

If we are not afraid to face and talk about dying, we would then say, "Do you feel like talking about it?"

As long as a patient is alive, he needs hope, but not the projection of our hope, which is usually a prolongation of life.

Besides the need for hope, patients need a reassurance that they will not be deserted, yet most of our patients who become beyond medical help feel deserted.

To give you a brief clinical example of what I mean by the loneliness of dying, I had a 28-year-old mother of three small children with liver disease. Because of her liver disease, she was going in and out of hepatic comas, and became frequently confused and psychotic.

Her husband could not take it any more. He had spent all his savings on doctor and hospital bills. He had these three little children. He had no homemaker, no help whatsoever. He was heavily in debt, and he never knew when he came home from work whether his wife was still functioning.

One day he said, "It would be better if you would live one single day and function as a housewife and a mother, rather than to prolong this misery any longer."

Unfortunately nobody helped this desperate husband and father, who tried unsuccessfully to provide for his family. The patient herself desperately looked for hope, which nobody gave her. She went to the hospital, where a young resident told her, "There is nothing else I can do for you."

She then went home, and in her desperation went to a faith healer, who told her that she was cured. She believed this, and stopped taking the medication, stopped taking the diet, and she again slipped into a coma.

Nobody helped this family. She was again admitted to the hospital. By then, the family had it. They just could not cope with it any more.

In the hospital, the same tragedy: The medical ward wanted to transfer her to the psychiatric ward, and the latter did not want a dying patient and insisted that she be kept on a medical floor. They could not tolerate this woman who walked up and down the hallway talking about God's miracles, of the faith healer who cured her.

It became like a Ping-Pong game, and this is the tragedy of hospitalized patients who cause all these anxieties in us. We don't know what to say or do with them.

I told this woman that I would never talk with her about her illness or dying, and I would not desert her. "Let's only talk about the present." She became the best patient I ever had, but she was put in the last room at the end of a long hallway, farthest away from the nursing station.

Not one door closed, but two doors. She never had a visitor.

This woman, when I visited with her one day, sat on the edge of the bed with the telephone off the hook in her hands. I said, "What in the world are you doing?" She said, "Oh, just to hear a sound!" This is the loneliness of the dying patients that I am talking about.

Another time, she was lying on her bed smiling, with her arms stiff down the side of her body and I asked her, "What in the world are you smiling about?" She looked at me and said, "Don't you see these beautiful flowers that my husband surrounded me with?" Needless to say, there were no flowers.

It took me a while to appreciate that this woman realized that she just could not live without some expression of love and care, hopefully coming from her husband. In order to live, this woman had to develop a delusion of flowers, sent to her by her husband after her death.

This is the loneliness I am talking about. And these things would be preventable if we would not hospitalize all these patients, but if we could give the family some help at the beginning, if we could occasionally relieve them with homemakers, if we could send physicians and caseworkers to their homes, so that this last hospitalization can be prevented, and the dying patient can at least die in his own home, surrounded by the children, and also in the familiar environment where they have lived, and where they have been loved. But in order to do this, we have to give help not only to the dying patient but to such desperate husbands who try to make ends meet and just cannot make it alone.

A Death-denying Society

We live in a very peculiar, death-denying society. We isolate both the dying and the old, and it serves a purpose, I guess. They are reminders of our own mortality.

Why do I bring up all these specific examples? I think we can do something about it. I think we have to put much more emphasis on education, on teaching even small children that death is part of life, or inviting old people who perhaps don't have a family any more into our homes, to take them in as grandmothers and grandfathers, not only to give them the final care, but to allow our children to have an experience of having old and sick people in our house.

We should not institutionalize people. We can give the families much more help with home care, visiting nurses, giving the families and the patient spiritual, emotional, and financial help in order to facilitate the final care at home.

We very badly need alternative living situations like smaller housing units in hometowns which are financially accessible, and I am not going to talk only about the dying patient. We need retirement villages, not isolated from the center of life, in a community for the healthy old people.

We need much more homemaker services, shopping services, delivery services, and much better medical services. Indeed, transportation to physicians, and more physicians who make house calls.

Nursing homes should be part of other facilities, not dead ends. Every nursing home, in my opinion, should have a day-care center on the premises, where the elderly, lonely person can become a grandparent to a lonely, needy child. It would take much less staff, it would cost less money, and it would also teach the young child that old age can be a source of wisdom and love, even when the eyesight fails and the steps slow down.

Children should be allowed and encouraged to visit mental institutions, old age homes, and hospitals, so that they grow up knowing that old age and death is part of life, just like birth is.

Starting Time		*Finishing Time*	
Reading Time		*Reading Rate*	
Comprehension		*Vocabulary*	

Comprehension— Read the following questions and statements. For each one, put an *x* in the box before the option that contains the most complete or accurate answer. Check your answers in the Answer Key on page 107.

1. A dying person has a profound need for
   □ a. hope and security.
   □ b. gifts and flowers.
   □ c. peace and solitude.
   □ d. rest and quiet.

2. The author's attitude toward death was molded by her
   □ a. surroundings.
   □ b. teachers.
   □ c. readings.
   □ d. research.

3. The 28-year-old woman with liver disease turned to a faith healer after
   □ a. her husband deserted her.
   □ b. doctors said they could do nothing more for her.
   □ c. the author began interviewing her.
   □ d. she was taken to a psychiatric hospital.

4. Death would be understood better if
   □ a. people looked upon death as a part of living.
   □ b. institutions for the elderly were properly staffed.
   □ c. mental patients were treated at home.
   □ d. doctors explained the stages of dying.

5. The transformation undergone by the young mother sick with cancer was
   □ a. hopeless.
   □ b. sorrowful.
   □ c. necessary and desirable.
   □ d. cruel and painful.

6. The author's concern for living with dignity rather than dying with dignity is
   □ a. surprising.   □ c. strange.
   □ b. positive.   □ d. unusual.

7. Children are not
   □ a. interested in death.
   □ b. affected by the death of their elders.
   □ c. encouraged to talk about death.
   □ d. able to deal with the concept of death.

8. The author's analysis and treatment of her subject is
   □ a. morbid.
   □ b. objective.
   □ c. demoralizing.
   □ d. sensitive.

9. The author is
   □ a. an appreciative woman.
   □ b. an incompetent doctor.
   □ c. a crusading liberal.
   □ d. a compassionate person.

10. The statement that treatment of the dying woman "became like a Ping-Pong game" is an example of
    □ a. a metaphor.
    □ b. a simile.
    □ c. literal language.
    □ d. alliteration.

Comprehension Skills	
1. recalling specific facts	6. making a judgment
2. retaining concepts	7. making an inference
3. organizing facts	8. recognizing tone
4. understanding the main idea	9. understanding characters
5. drawing a conclusion	10. appreciation of literary forms

Study Skills, Part One—Following is a passage with blanks where words have been omitted. Next to the passage are groups of five words, one group for each blank. Complete the passage by selecting the correct word for each of the blanks.

The Therefore Paragraph

The next pattern of paragraph development we want to examine is called the Therefore. It is used anytime the author wishes to present ___(1)___ steps to an argument or a conclusion. The author's purpose is persuasion—the pattern is to lead you logically to the conclusion by presenting the successive ___(2)___ that it is based on.

Graphically the Therefore looks like this:

STEPS
LEADING
TO
CONCLUSION

(1)   various   interesting
    successful   deviating   successive

(2)   promises   occasions
    premises   guesses   hopes

Here is an example of the Therefore:

In any event many skills and habits cannot be gained without ___(3)___ . But practice itself may be blundering, incidental, and accidental; or it may be intelligent, formal, and planned. Life is too short, and time too limited to be spent in ___(4)___ trial and error practice.

(therefore)

This is why we have ___(5)___ , for it is under directed, regular, and supervised drill that students most rapidly acquire proper mental habits.

In the Therefore pattern, the reader is led logically to the author's ___(6)___ . The evidence is there; you have no alternative but to accept the logical statement that follows.

In textbooks, this pattern is used to demonstrate the ___(7)___ of certain principles of the subject.

(3)   punctuality   desire
      practice   purpose   destiny

(4)   necessary   wasteful
      helpful   hasty   unskilled

(5)   churches   schools
      markets   libraries   museums

(6)   belief   conclusion
      theory   revelation   decision

(7)   veracity   variety
      validity   virility   victory

Study Skills, Part Two—Read the study skills passage again, paying special attention to the lesson being taught. Then, without looking back at the passage, complete each sentence below by writing in the missing word or words. Check the Answer Key on page 107 for the answers to Study Skills, Part One, and Study Skills, Part Two.

1. The author's purpose in the Therefore paragraph is _____ .

2. The Therefore paragraph consists of steps _____ logically to a conclusion.

3. In the sample paragraph, the author maintains that regular practice and drill result in proper mental _____ .

4. The Therefore paragraph presents the reader with evidence that gives him no _____ but to accept the statement that follows.

5. This pattern is used in textbooks to prove that certain principles of the subject are _____ .

Something's Happening Out There

by Charles Kuralt

Vocabulary—The five words below are from the story you are about to read. Study the words and their meanings. Then complete the ten sentences that follow, using one of the five words to fill in the blank in each sentence. Mark your answer by writing the letter of the word on the line before the sentence. Check your answers in the Answer Key on page 107.

A. perceptibly: noticeably

B. grotesque: bizarre; ugly; distorted

C. aberrations: unusual elements; deviations

D. mesmerized: hypnotized

E. impetus: driving force

_____ 1. The _____ behind the author's journey was a desire to examine America's true spirit.

_____ 2. The number of young people involved in politics has increased _____ .

_____ 3. The author sought out ordinary citizens, not society's _____ .

_____ 4. Louisiana teacher Andy Spirer can alter _____ the future of a few young students.

_____ 5. The author believes that fascists are real _____ in this country.

_____ 6. Frieda Klussman provided the _____ needed to save San Francisco's cable cars.

_____ 7. Racism is a _____ distortion of American values.

_____ 8. For many years, images of the Vietnam War _____ the viewers of network news.

_____ 9. The author was _____ by the stories of ordinary Americans.

_____ 10. _____ incidents of racial abuse have not destroyed the author's faith in America.

Shed a tear for the passing of the dream. America has become computerized, plastic, impersonal. Americans have grown guilty, isolated, rootless. We are so accustomed to hearing those things about ourselves that we've come to believe them.

Well, I don't believe them any more! I've been wandering through the great cities and down the back roads

The popular CBS television reporter talks of what he has learned during his years of traveling across the USA.

of the United States and, much to my surprise, I've come to know a country that's as sturdy as a New England fishing boat and as lively as a Georgia fiddle tune.

Her brooding "silent majority" is not silent at all; it is talking all the time—questioning, debating with neighbors over the back fence, and clamoring for attention on the radio telephone-talk shows.

Her "alienated" youth are, in fact, far more deeply involved in the raucous give and take of the democratic system than any other youthful generation in our history; half of them, it sometimes seemed to me this summer, were out ringing doorbells for Presidential candidates.

Her "oppressed" minorities, who still carry the unfair burden of centuries of discrimination and neglect, have felt that burden lightening perceptibly; few black Americans, or Mexican-Americans, or Puerto Ricans will tell you they see anything but hope in the turbulent events of recent years.

Of course, I know America has perplexing, knotty problems. I haven't been traveling the country with my eyes closed. Along the way, I've heard the ignorant words of racial abuse. I've seen the cities' slums and the migrant workers' shacks. I've seen the scattered, ugly signs of financial greed, the hillsides skinned by strip miners, the forests ravished by clear-cutters, the grotesque billboard alleys some of our roadways have become. And in some café beside a highway some mornings, I've read the calamitous headlines about drug addiction and war in distant places.

What saves me from despair is that, after reading about these aberrations in our national life, I fold the morning paper and step outside the café into our national life itself. The country of the headlines, which seems so insane and homicidal, gives way to the real country, where there are many strengths the headline writers have no space to describe.

I look in vain for all the disaffected people, poisoned by the networks, radicalized by the universities, and dealing in narcotics on the side. What I find instead, at every hand, are people whose lives are lived in satisfying peace with their neighbors, who treat wayfaring strangers with open-handed friendliness and who remain stubbornly hopeful about their country. Most of them believe in America's essential fairness, and most of them are far from indifferent to America's many wounds. Lately, increasingly, I've found them willing to take a part, themselves, in binding up those wounds. Eric Sevareid told me once that there is such a

thing as a national conscience in the United States, and that it can be felt more profoundly here than anywhere else in the world. I didn't know quite what he meant until I started traveling.

Faces come back to me in close-up—a few of the people I've met on the road.

I remember the roughhewn face of Andy Spirer, bent over a desk in the Pilottown, Louisiana, public school, teaching first-grader Kevin Nelson how to make the letter "M." Andy Spirer went to college on the G.I. Bill expressly for the purpose of teaching in Pilottown, which didn't have a teacher. It did have three pupils, and I found Andy Spirer teaching them, gently, lovingly, in a one-room school in a town without roads, isolated at the mouth of the Mississippi. He explained, "Sure, I get lonely here, but it's worth it. I try to give each child every bit of knowledge I've learned in the book world, in the social world, in the physical world. They have to go up the river to high school when they get old enough. Part of my pride goes with them, see, so that makes it worthwhile."

Without Andy Spirer, where would we be? But don't look for his name on the front pages.

The serene, aristocratic face of Frieda Klussman pops into my memory. She is riding a cable car in San Francisco, admiring her city from her alfresco perch. When city officials tried to replace the cable cars with buses, it was Mrs. Klussman who marched out of her hilltop mansion, rolled up her sleeves, organized her friends, and went to war. "You can put a hundred people on a cable car and you have a feeling of camaraderie among them," she told me. "You hear laughter. Put these same people on a bus, and everybody is grouchy and grumpy. We *had* to save the cable cars!"

There's a rockbound guarantee in the City Charter of San Francisco that cable cars will go on forever. Frieda Klussman got it there, though hardly anyone who rides the cable cars today has any way of knowing that.

Unselfish Couple

And here is the dark, intense face of Rumel Fuentes and the contrasting, smiling face of Jo Fuentes at work on the neighborhood center in Eagle Pass, Texas. He's a young Mexican-American. She is his wife, a girl from Ohio who had never seen a Mexican-American until she came to Eagle Pass as a Vista Volunteer. When I met them, Jo, a Catholic, was running the Planned Parenthood Center, because *somebody* had to run the Planned Parenthood Center. In the afternoons, she worked as secretary at the Methodist Church. Saturdays, she had the Girl Scout troop. Rumel Fuentes got up before dawn each morning to ride 60 miles to the nearest college. Monday, Wednesday, and Friday nights, he was teaching American citizenship classes. Tuesday, Thursday, and Saturday nights, he was teaching high school classes for dropouts. Sundays, the Fuenteses worked on the neighborhood center, which was their idea, and which the people in the community were paying for with money from the sale of tamales and old clothes. The Fuenteses thought that some things were wrong in Eagle Pass, and that they could improve them. They knew they could live better elsewhere, but they planned to stay.

I'm persuaded that there are more such faces in America than there were even a few short years ago. Writer George Orwell, who predicted a nation of robots, marching to the tick of a Big Government metronome, reckoned without the little surprises of which the American spirit is capable. Today, many of the best young law school graduates are hanging out their shingles on ghetto storefronts, and *cum laude* products of Ivy League business schools are questioning potential employers about their attitude toward the environment before agreeing to go to work.

I have the advantage over those who foresee that Americans will soon become robots—the advantage of looking into their faces.

Created a Park

And the pretty, dirt-smudged face of Pat Baker, a young, white mother of three who was told there was no money to turn a vacant lot in a black neighborhood of Reno, Nevada, into a park. So she organized a breathtaking community effort to do exactly that, and in 48 hours of one remarkable weekend, a park—with basketball courts, paved paths, benches, green grass, and trees—came true.

And the gentle face of Paul Crews, county agent in Suwannee County, Florida, who perceived that what the poorest black farmers in the region needed were breeding stock and advice, which the most prosperous white farmers could give. So he sat them all down to have barbecue, beans, and cole slaw together and, getting to know one another, white and black farmers in Suwannee County found themselves beginning to care about one another.

I remember the strong, black face of Larry Brooks, whose burglary career sent him to prison, and who, when he got out on parole, decided on a new career—parole officer. "See," he said, "parole officers don't know enough about what's going on in the head of the parolee, all the things he's worried about, his family, and finding a job, staying out of trouble. See, *I know.*" Parole officials agreed Larry Brooks was one of the best they'd ever seen, good enough that he'd be getting off parole pretty soon himself.

I remember the face of old Walter Misenheimer, who worked for years after he retired at the age of 70 to convert a wasted, grown-over woodlot beside his house in Virginia into an exquisite 13-acre garden, just so tourists passing by would have a place to stretch their legs and enjoy the beauty of dogwood and azaleas.

As these faces of ordinary Americans have accumulated in my experience, the strident axioms about "guilty," "conformist," "materialistic" Americans that I used to half-accept as true have come to seem wildly inapplicable to the observable America before me. And those stronger words, "fascist," "criminal," and "repressive," which are used by the most bitterly critical writers of the underground press to describe the country, I can only understand as a view from Oz, where words had no meaning. After all, Oz was also underground.

National Problems Being Solved

Out in the light of day, Americans no longer seem mesmerized by their national problems. Somewhere in the course of our recent history, very many of them have shrugged off the hesitancy and doubt which characterized the country's mood and regained their old, jaunty certainty that for every problem, there is a solution. They are, as often before, well ahead of their leaders; the impetus for ending the Vietnam War, for revising the tax structure, for cleaning up the environment, did not originate in the White House or Congress but out there among the people.

In Tarentum, Pennsylvania, this year, I remarked on the beauty of the riverbanks, and discovered it is an organization of the town's kids who keep them that way. In Dayton, Ohio, the kids took over an old gasoline station and made it into a citywide recycling center. In Marin County, California, the kids reclaimed a marsh from beer cans and garbage and turned it into a school nature-study project. Hardly a town in the country is without a similar example of sensitivity to "ecology"—even though the word was unknown to all but a handful of worried specialists a few years ago.

A woman who is one of Somerset, Wisconsin's leading citizens revealed herself to me recently as an ardent ally of the women's liberation movement. "I got tired of sitting around the house," she said. "I just saw there were some things I could do, and I've been doing them. And since this spring, I've even been *talking* about it!"

I can remember very well a time when *nobody* talked about improving the status of women. Now, they're talking about it in little towns in Wisconsin.

No doubt, the present openness of the American mind—and mouth—owes much to the likes of Martin Luther King and Ralph Nader and Cesar Chavez, who, though largely unknown, spoke up against injustices in a quieter time. Now, the country is abuzz with the issues they raised, and many others, too—on the farm no less than on the campus.

This spirited debate about every national issue from busing to big business is a wonderful thing, I think, a renewal of what used to be called "patriotism"—concern for one's country. It was Jefferson who said, "Enlighten the people generally, and tyranny and oppressions of body and mind will vanish like evil spirits at the dawn of day." Rest easy, Mr. Jefferson. The people generally are busy enlightening one another.

I know some people fear we are being destroyed by all this clamor. I am of the opposite view: We're being revitalized by it. America's weaknesses and contradictions are out in the open for the world to see. Americans themselves have been the first to see them. Wherever I have gone, I have found Americans hard at work on their resolution.

Those faces keep coming back to me. They are all right, those faces. They are unsullied by false superiority or hostility toward other people or any selfish motive, and they are numberless in my memory. They give me reason to hope that our country is growing, not just in size and wealth, but in wisdom and humanity, too.

Starting Time		*Finishing Time*	
Reading Time		*Reading Rate*	
Comprehension		*Vocabulary*	

Comprehension— Read the following questions and statements. For each one, put an *x* in the box before the option that contains the most complete or accurate answer. Check your answers in the Answer Key on page 107.

1. The author's travels took him
   - ☐ a. only to small towns and villages.
   - ☐ b. to every city in America.
   - ☐ c. from coast to coast.
   - ☐ d. to the bleakest and most depressing spots in the country.

2. George Orwell had not counted on America's
   - ☐ a. ability to bounce back.
   - ☐ b. social and racial problems.
   - ☐ c. rapid economic expansion.
   - ☐ d. schools of higher learning.

3. The author reached his conclusions about America
   - ☐ a. while reporting on the Vietnam War.
   - ☐ b. long before he hit the road.
   - ☐ c. as a result of his travels.
   - ☐ d. after studying the writings of Thomas Jefferson.

4. America has reason to have confidence in itself as a nation especially if it considers its
   - ☐ a. great human resources.
   - ☐ b. abundant natural wealth.
   - ☐ c. powerful military position.
   - ☐ d. democratic way of life.

5. Americans, it seems, have a tendency to
   - ☐ a. overlook their obvious shortcomings.
   - ☐ b. corrupt everything they touch.
   - ☐ c. isolate themselves from others.
   - ☐ d. criticize themselves severely.

6. The average American
   - ☐ a. is a power to be considered.
   - ☐ b. is a helpless victim of circumstances.
   - ☐ c. makes unreasonable demands.
   - ☐ d. misunderstands the national issues.

7. The author believes that Americans
   - ☐ a. have become computerized.
   - ☐ b. have grown guilty.
   - ☐ c. are a silent majority.
   - ☐ d. are a vital people.

8. The tone of the selection is
   - ☐ a. discouraging.
   - ☐ c. insulting.
   - ☐ b. optimistic.
   - ☐ d. self-satisfied.

9. A characteristic shared by the people referred to in the selection is
   - ☐ a. an unusual degree of arrogance.
   - ☐ b. a basic distrust in America's future.
   - ☐ c. a definite tendency toward conformity.
   - ☐ d. a strong sense of responsibility.

10. The author develops his theme by using
   - ☐ a. dialogue.
   - ☐ c. examples.
   - ☐ b. questions.
   - ☐ d. symbols.

Comprehension Skills

1. recalling specific facts	6. making a judgment
2. retaining concepts	7. making an inference
3. organizing facts	8. recognizing tone
4. understanding the main idea	9. understanding characters
5. drawing a conclusion	10. appreciation of literary forms

Study Skills, Part One—Following is a passage with blanks where words have been omitted. Next to the passage are groups of five words, one group for each blank. Complete the passage by selecting the correct word for each of the blanks.

The Proceeder Paragraph

The next pattern of paragraph development we wish to examine is the Proceeder. This paragraph ___(1)___ on

(1) builds depends
    descends develops thrives

successive facts, proceeding from the lesser to the greater point until the main idea is developed. It proceeds from the specific to the ___(2)___ .

Graphically the Proceeder looks like this:

SPECIFIC
GENERAL
MORE GENERAL
MAIN IDEA

Here is an example of the Proceeder:

The Freshman is fairly sure that he knows many things quite well. The Sophomore is absolutely ___(3)___ that he knows most things very well. The Junior has begun to have serious doubts about the quantity and quality of what he knows. The Senior is quite convinced that he knows almost nothing about anything. Then he graduates and tries to get an employer to pay him for what he ___(4)___ .

This pattern is different from the others we have been examining in that the main idea statement is not the inclusive ___(5)___ that it is in the others. The statement here is simply a broader or more general concept that the preceding ones have been expanded into.

Its value to the reader is that it encourages acceptance of the general statement. The reader has been able to see it ___(6)___ and build from its humble beginnings.

In textbooks this pattern will be employed when the author has to present ___(7)___ concepts to the student and wishes to lead the student progressively to them.

(2)   great   generous   narrow   general   significant

(3)   hopeful   definite   certain   unsure   specific

(4)   declares   believes   learns   attempts   knows

(5)   emancipation   socialization   generalization   organization   speculation

(6)   falter   continue   progress   ascend   improve

(7)   binding   beneficial   broad   basic   believable

Study Skills, Part Two—Read the study skills passage again, paying special attention to the lesson being taught. Then, without looking back at the passage, complete each sentence below by writing in the missing word or words. Check the Answer Key on page 107 for the answers to Study Skills, Part One, and Study Skills, Part Two.

1. The Proceeder paragraph progresses from the _____ to the greater point.

2. The facts get broader until the main idea is _____ .

3. According to the sample paragraph, the Freshman student thinks he knows a lot, but the Senior student thinks he know _____ .

4. This pattern is different from the others because the main idea is not an _____ generalization.

5. The author uses this kind of paragraph to lead the reader progressively to the presentation of a broad _____ .

10 | **Tell-Tale Stones,
Old Bones**

by Walter Olesky

Vocabulary—The five words below are from the story you are about to read. Study the words and their meanings. Then complete the ten sentences that follow, using one of the five words to fill in the blank in each sentence. Mark your answer by writing the letter of the word on the line before the sentence. Check your answers in the Answer Key on page 107.

A. meticulous: very careful

B. sedentary: settled; not migratory

C. hedonistic: pleasure-seeking

D. lucrative: profitable

E. devastating: destructive

_____ 1. Permanent dwellings are one sign of a _____ society.

_____ 2. Carol Stitzer found that teaching kindergarten was more _____ than working at the Koster site.

_____ 3. Successful archaeologists must exhibit a _____ attention to detail.

_____ 4. Warfare with a hostile tribe was often _____ to a prehistoric civilization.

_____ 5. Archaeologists now have evidence that some hunter-gatherer societies lived a _____ life.

_____ 6. Not all young people crave a wild, _____ existence.

_____ 7. A careless worker can have a _____ effect on an archaeological dig.

_____ 8. Nancy Dietz proved to be a _____ worker.

_____ 9. Early hunter-gatherer societies had too many worries and too many responsibilities to live a _____ life.

_____ 10. There are more _____ ways to spend a summer than working on the Koster farm.

Digging into the past gave these students a fresh fix on the future.

Above, the hot August sun drenches the farmland along the lower Illinois River valley near Kampsville, a town about forty-five miles north of St. Louis. Except for a gopher that darts between the cornstalks and a crow circling overhead, there appears to be no sign of life on this remote stretch of Illinois prairie.

Appearances are deceiving. Fifteen feet below the surface, in a hole six feet square, a slim, barefoot high school senior from Evanston, Illinois, is kneeling on the cool ground. She wears a sweatshirt and cutoffs, and a red bandanna protects her blonde hair from falling dirt. Her arms are weary from hours of painstaking, arduous labor.

A labor of love, however. Nancy Dietz is one of almost 200 amateur, volunteer archaeologists helping a team of scientists probe what may be the most important archaeological excavation in North America—thirty acres of the Theodore Koster farm in Greene County, Illinois. Nancy applies her trowel with meticulous care to loosen the clay and dirt, watchful for any evidence that human beings might once have lived where she is digging.

The job calls for concentration and patience—intense patience. Most of the day has gone, and Nancy has scarcely a dozen buckets of stony dirt to show for her efforts. But quality counts, not quantity, when you are sifting centuries and the objects you must not damage or overlook can be as small as a corn seed or as inconspicuous as a tiny fragment of flint.

Nancy signals for another loaded bucket to be raised topside for inspection. Earl Carlson, an instructor in combined studies at Evanston Township High School, cranks up the bucket and prepares to examine the collected debris.

Although it looks like hundreds of other piles of dirt he has screened to catch fragments of pottery or utensils, Carlson remains alert, for other relics found nearby prove that ancient man did live in this fertile valley. Picking over the dirt, Carlson notices something that might be a pointed piece of rock. Or, perhaps, a stone deliberately shaped into a point?

Carlson calls another supervisor to inspect the object. Their excitement rises as they realize that it is an Agate Basin projectile, part of a tool used by prehistoric man for either hunting or grinding. It's made of chert, an extremely hard crystalline rock. From the depth at which Nancy was working they estimate that a human hand held the stone some 7,000 years before the Christian era.

The discovery becomes the big news of the day when Nancy, Earl Carlson, and their co-workers return to base camp at Kampsville later that afternoon. There the projectile point is hailed as the oldest object yet found in the excavation of the Koster site.

Since the summer of 1968, remains of fifteen prehistoric civilizations have been found in layers down through thirty-five feet of soil on this section of the Koster farm. Koster and his wife have surrendered the acreage to science and amiably put up with not only some 300 scientists and student volunteers digging the land in search of ancient relics, but nearly 30,000 curious visitors each summer. Northwestern University and the Foundation for Illinois Archaeology sponsor the Koster dig, and more than two-thirds of the excavation budget is raised through public subscription.

There's abundant evidence at Koster to prove that man lived and hunted or farmed in the valley on and off from 7000 B.C. to 1200 A.D. Animal and human skeletons have been found there, including those of an infant who died 7,000 years ago and a dog believed to have been a domestic pet a century earlier, along with pottery, tools, hunting equipment, cooking utensils, and petrified corn pollen. Indians were in the Koster area long before Druids raised the Stonehenge monoliths (1800 B.C.) or slave labor constructed the Egyptian pyramids (3000 B.C.).

Even more important to archaeologists than Nancy's ancient chert point was the discovery of remnants of four permanent dwellings containing hearths and storage pits. It is estimated that the structures, the earliest habitations yet discovered in North America, were occupied by prehistoric man more than 6,000 years ago. Found at a depth of thirty-four feet, they have caused much discussion.

Remains of large post holes suggest that the structures were substantial and perhaps used year-round. They predate by 1,500 years evidence of other ancient dwellings found at Koster in 1972 as well as a cemetery containing twenty skeletons, mostly of adolescents. (The oldest signs of man in North America are at Clovis, New Mexico, and are dated at 9500 B.C., but no evidence has revealed any dwellings.)

"The discovery that Indians living in Illinois more than 6,000 years ago were sophisticated enough to alter the landscape and put up substantial structures changes some of our ideas about early man," says Dr. Stuart Struever, a professor of anthropology and archaeology at Northwestern University and director of the excavation activities.

"We used to think that permanent villages and a sedentary life only came about after people had developed agriculture," Struever explains. "But in the lower Illinois valley agriculture did not become a way of life until several hundred years after the birth of Christ. These ancient houses were built by people who relied on a hunting and gathering economy."

Several features of the Koster dig help explain why it has become one of the most important North American archaeological sites. Most significant is that each period of habitation is located in a clearly defined layer of evidence; scientists call these strata "horizons." The distance between layers indicates that this fertile valley was not continuously occupied. A settlement might endure for several hundred years, according to present scientific speculation. Then the inhabitants would depart and not be replaced by new immigrants for a similar period. This pattern, the evidence suggests, continued over thousands of years. In between habitations, earth, washed down from the slopes surrounding the valley, would fill in and cover the previous settlement. Furthermore, the soil's high alkali content helped keep the animal and plant remains in a remarkable state of preservation over the millenia.

Struever came upon this rich prehistoric trove in the summer of 1968 while looking for Indian pottery fragments in the area. He found not only pottery but the remains of a Jersey Bluff Indian settlement from the period 800 to 1200 A.D. Since then, Struever has returned each summer with a cadre of scientists and a small army of youthful assistants who range in age from fourteen to the mid-twenties.

A number of local stores and shops have been converted into laboratories. Here the scientists, from various universities, inspect and catalog the day's findings, delivered to them by the students on their return to town. Several nights a week the student assistants gather at the church hall to hear Struever and other authorities discuss various phases of the project.

Unpaid, uncomfortable labor, digging for the bones and relics of people long dead, is hardly orthodox activity for a youthful generation often described as selfish and hedonistic. What draws these particular young people to it?

"I volunteered to dig at Koster last summer because a friend who dug there the year before told me it was exciting," Nancy Dietz explains. "It was hard work but exciting, too. Especially when I sent up that bucket with the chert projectile."

Wendy Wolf, Nancy's friend and also from Evanston, worked at Koster for two weeks one year and returned for the full summer the next year. She says she has always been interested in people and their cultures. "What I've learned here has made me decide to major in anthropology or archaeology in college," she comments.

Peter Fritzsche, fourteen, an intense, articulate freshman at the University of Chicago Lab School, also worked the full summer at Koster last year, after spending a week there the two previous summers. He helped uncover remains of the earliest houses found so far.

Mary Etzkorn, from Chicago, completed her sophomore year at Mundelein College, then decided to take a vacation from classroom work and volunteered to dig in the fields at Koster last summer. When she arrived in early June, the valley and Kampsville were practically buried under mud from heavy spring rains. She joined the others in cleaning up the site and the houses and laboratories in town.

"Ever since I was a kid, I wanted to be an archaeologist," says Mary. "I figured that you learn best by doing something, so I quit college for a year. I came to Koster partly to see if I could hack the hard work. I learned that I could take it."

Carol Stitzer is a thirty-year-old former kindergarten teacher who left a lucrative and comfortable job with a Chicago market research firm to come to Koster last summer and do what most interested her—archaeology. She was involved in work at Horizon 8, a level some twenty feet below the surface that yielded a wide variety of artifacts, prominent among them an ancient grinding stone.

"I'm both scientifically and artistically oriented, and archaeology has a little of each in it," says Carol. "It's exciting to me and I like to work outdoors. And I've gotten valuable field experience that will help me when I do graduate work in archaeology. There were times, when I was knee-deep in mud helping clean up the site after the floods, when I thought I must be sick in the head. But I'm going back this summer, and this time I hope to learn the lab side of the project."

Dr. Struever looks somewhat deeper for the reason why working at Koster appeals to the young people. "They're naturally restless," he says, "and I believe archaeology helps them to develop deep ground roots. Working with their hands, digging in the ground, unearthing the mysteries of past civilizations seems to give them a sense of continuity. Their world is threatened by war and the Bomb. On the Koster farm, they come to realize that ancient man had to face equally devastating threats to his civilization, from warfare on a very personal level to famine, predatory animals, and natural disasters such as floods and the Ice Age."

His usually animated face grows more still and serious. He adds, "The fifteen civilizations which settled at various times in the Illinois River valley prove that man endures. New life comes back. And for archaeologists and young adventurers alike, it's almost too incredible to believe that such rich prehistory is buried so close to home. Not in Egypt, but right here in Southern Illinois."

Starting Time		Finishing Time	
Reading Time		Reading Rate	
Comprehension		Vocabulary	

Comprehension— Read the following questions and statements. For each one,
put an *x* in the box before the option that contains the most complete or
accurate answer. Check your answers in the Answer Key on page 107.

1. The finds made at the Koster site have been well
   preserved by the
   ☐ a. ingenuity of early man.
   ☐ b. cold climate of the area.
   ☐ c. high alkali content of the soil.
   ☐ d. patience and care of archaeologists.

2. The site of the Koster farm is
   ☐ a. centrally located.
   ☐ b. rich in minerals.
   ☐ c. economically depressed.
   ☐ d. steeped in history.

3. Which of the following have not been found at
   the Koster site?
   ☐ a. a chert point
   ☐ b. the remains of storage pits
   ☐ c. human skeletons
   ☐ d. cave drawings

4. The selection illustrates
   ☐ a. man's pursuit of his origin.
   ☐ b. the influence of science.
   ☐ c. man's will to survive.
   ☐ d. the importance of agriculture.

5. Involvement in archaeological digs can give people
   ☐ a. a fear of the past.
   ☐ b. financial security.
   ☐ c. a sense of perspective.
   ☐ d. mysterious diseases.

6. The discoveries made by archaeologists can be
   looked upon as
   ☐ a. signs of things to come.
   ☐ b. status symbols.
   ☐ c. windows into the past.
   ☐ d. common objects.

7. Evidence suggests that the people whose remains were
   found in Clovis, New Mexico, were probably
   ☐ a. warriors.
   ☐ b. nomads.
   ☐ c. farmers.
   ☐ d. merchants.

8. The atmosphere in the opening paragraph is
   ☐ a. serene.
   ☐ b. tense.
   ☐ c. troubled.
   ☐ d. comical.

9. Nancy Dietz seems
   ☐ a. intent and dedicated.
   ☐ b. confused.
   ☐ c. lonely.
   ☐ d. impatient and aggravated.

10. The author emphasizes the dedication of the
    volunteers by using
    ☐ a. symbolism.
    ☐ b. figurative language.
    ☐ c. understatement.
    ☐ d. direct quotations.

Comprehension Skills	
1. recalling specific facts	*6. making a judgment*
2. retaining concepts	*7. making an inference*
3. organizing facts	*8. recognizing tone*
4. understanding the main idea	*9. understanding characters*
5. drawing a conclusion	*10. appreciation of literary forms*

Study Skills, Part One—Following is a passage with blanks where words have
been omitted. Next to the passage are groups of five words, one group for
each blank. Complete the passage by selecting the correct word for each of
the blanks.

The For Example Paragraph

   The fifth pattern of paragraph development is called the
For Example. It is a(n) ___(1)___ of the Fable paragraph—
the main idea or generalization comes first, followed by
the illustration or story.

(1)   inversion   intervention
        conversion   convention   diversion

Graphically the For Example looks like this:

MAIN IDEA
STORY
OR
ILLUSTRATION

Here is an example of the For Example:

Conversationalists of the low-level or high-level variety are uniformly dull. As Wendell Johnson observes: "The low-level speaker ___(2)___ you because he leaves you with no directions as to what to do with the basketful of ___(3)___ given to you. The high-level speaker frustrates you because he simply doesn't tell you what he is ___(4)___ about— being thus frustrated, and being further blocked because the rules of courtesy (or of attendance at class lectures) ___(5)___ that one remain quietly seated until the speaker has finished, there is little for one to do but daydream, doodle, or simply fall asleep."

Like the Fable, this pattern presents a story or ___(6)___ to illustrate the main point. Observe too that there are no facts or data presented in the illustration for the student to digest and ___(7)___ . The story is there simply to help the reader get the point.

(2) encourages   discourages
     frustrates   excites   interests

(3) integration   confrontation
     summation   formation   information

(4) worrying   thinking
     talking   boasting   complaining

(5) forbid   require
     suggest   urge   propose

(6) essay   ballad
     sonnet   anecdote   myth

(7) forget   memorize
     study   reject   retain

Study Skills, Part Two—Read the study skills passage again, paying special attention to the lesson being taught. Then, without looking back at the passage, complete each sentence below by writing in the missing word or words. Check the Answer Key on page 107 for the answers to Study Skills, Part One, and Study Skills, Part Two.

1. In the For Example paragraph, the main idea comes at the

   _____ .

2. The story or illustration comes at the _____ .

3. The main idea of the sample paragraph states that high- and low-level

   conversationalists share the quality of being _____ .

4. Like the Fable paragraph, this kind of paragraph presents a story to

   _____ the main point.

5. The story does not contain important _____ for the student

   to learn.

11 The Great American Vandal

by John Keats

Vocabulary—The five words below are from the story you are about to read. Study the words and their meanings. Then complete the ten sentences that follow, using one of the five words to fill in the blank in each sentence. Mark your answer by writing the letter of the word on the line before the sentence. Check your answers in the Answer Key on page 107.

A. pursuit: search

B. dismantled: took apart

C. condoned: excused; forgave

D. affluent: wealthy

E. opulent: lavish; luxurious

_____ 1. Each year thousands of American tourists set off in _____ of souvenirs.

_____ 2. The actions of rude, thoughtless tourists should not be _____ .

_____ 3. Even the _____ among us often dress as though oppressed by poverty.

_____ 4. Even the most _____ hotels in Europe now use cheap generic silverware.

_____ 5. Refined individuals have never _____ the actions of loud, self-centered Americans.

_____ 6. Because *The Spirt of St. Louis* hangs from the ceiling, it has not been marred or _____ by tourists.

_____ 7. The _____ of vandals by police and other officials has apparently done nothing to stem the tide of destruction at our national parks and museums.

_____ 8. The _____ furnishings of many public buildings have been damaged by greedy visitors.

_____ 9. Some visitors have even _____ lights and bathroom fixtures in an attempt to take home a souvenir.

_____ 10. _____ tourists are not necessarily well-behaved tourists.

The American tourist in full pursuit of life, liberty, and happiness may be less dangerous to the civilized world than Attila, but not much. The recent destruction at the John F. Kennedy Center for the Performing Arts in Washington, D.C., provides an example of what occurs, on only slightly less dramatic levels, everywhere else our fun-loving friends and neighbors go.

It was American visitors, and no one else, who ground out their cigarettes in the carpets, who dismantled the chandeliers, pried the faucets off the bathroom basins and the brass covers off the electric outlets, who stole the silverware from the restaurants and the paintings from the walls, who cut swatches out of the carpets and draperies to take home for souvenirs. They took everything that was not nailed down and much else that was. It was again American visitors, and no one else, who stood around watching $1,500,000 worth of damage being done and did nothing to stop it.

The appalling thing was not that theft and wanton destruction were openly perpetrated and silently condoned by thousands of our countrymen. It was the vacuous stupidity of it all. Apparently no one had the slightest consideration for, or interest in, anyone else. No one thought that everything taken or defaced made the Center that much less attractive for the next fellow. The fact that the Center was not theirs to wreck made no impression on our native vulgarians. They were merely doing what came naturally to them.

They were, root and branch, of the same stock who think they can go barefoot into the shops of Orleans, Massachusetts, on Cape Cod, and steal from the counters. They do not go barefoot and steal because they are poor. Indeed, they are affluent. Presumably they do not go about in a state of undress committing crimes in their home towns, but they certainly do in towns like New Hope, Pennsylvania, where a family backed their station wagon to the entrance of the Playhouse Inn, the better to load it with all the fruit from a buffet table.

Our neighbors leave their spoor everywhere. In a national park in Utah, a vacationing family calmly tossed a large plastic bag of garbage onto the highway from their moving Cadillac, practically at the feet of an astonished National Park Service Ranger. At Perry's Victory Memorial on South Bass Island in Lake Erie, freedom-loving vacationers customarily smash their whiskey bottles against the granite shaft. At the Lincoln Boyhood National Memorial there is a bronze cast of the hearthstone, and lower logs of the original cabin sitting in a slight depression in the ground. One group of patriots used it for a latrine, leaving it strewn with feces and toilet paper.

God sheds His grace on America. What did you shed? Candy wrapper? Beer can? Bag of garbage?

In Yellowstone Park, several geysers and the Morning Glory Pool have been irretrievably lost, because interested tourists could not resist the temptation to clog the vents with coins, stones, and logs. It was nature-loving Mom, Pop, and the kids who sprayed their names on rocks in the Grand Canyon with paint they had bought for the purpose, and when a Ranger protested, the father coolly replied, "We thought this was what everybody did. The rocks are for everybody, aren't they?"

More serious than this routine swinishness is the destruction our nature-loving countrymen visit upon everything that makes a park worth visiting. With an aplomb that can only be imagined, tourists in recent years have loaded literally tons of fossil wood into the trunks of their automobiles; each year, the Park Service says, there is less and less of Arizona's petrified forest to be seen.

It is American tourists, and no one else who, floating down the Colorado River, have turned it and Lake Mead into a sewer. Instead of availing themselves of the facilities that have been so expensively provided for their use, the happy boaters simply relieve themselves into the water, or along the banks of the river.

A possibly more disgusting, and certainly more pathetic, example of sheer poverty of mind and soul is the destruction of our rare petroglyphs. These are Indian paintings on rock faces. There are several in the western parks, most notably at Mesa Verde, Colorado, and Canyon de Chelly, Arizona. Not content to gaze with wonder upon these evidences of our vanished past, tourists have sought to improve upon them with aerosol paint sprays, knives, hatchets, sharp stones, and, in one case, with rifle fire.

In additional to our national parks, historic sites and museums are particular targets of our touring barbarians—which accounts for the fact that so much of America's heritage is behind velvet ropes and iron bars or in glass cases, and is only to be seen through a screen of uniformed guards. It is not just for decorative effect that the Wright brothers' airplane and Lindbergh's *Spirit of St. Louis* are suspended from the Smithsonian Insitution's ceiling.

"There is almost nothing you can pick up and go away with now at our historical sites," a security officer at Independence Hall rather proudly said. "Of course, nobody can carry the Liberty Bell away, and they can't get close to the silver inkwells in the Assembly Room because we won't let them inside there. We make sure they can't get close to anything that is moveable. At the same time, we give them something they can take away. If they touch the Liberty Bell, they get a certificate, suitable for framing, that says they have made a pilgrimage to the cradle of the nation's liberty, and this helps to keep them from trying to steal something else."

The cost of saving public treasures from the American public can sometimes be more than a city can bear. In Philadelphia, there are no longer sufficient funds to provide guards enough for the Museum of Art. As a result, on any given day only certain galleries are open.

Depredation is still largely a function of distance. The farther from home he is, the more oafish the American oaf dares to become. But it is all coming closer, and the thieves and vandals are increasingly those one might suspect of knowing better. A friend who had always opened his colonial mansion in Maryland to the local ladies' spring garden club tour, at so much per head for sweet charity, unwittingly donated more than $2,500 last year to the ladies—in the form of the books they took from his library, the Picasso ashtrays from his study, the antique flatware from his dining room. The gentlewomen also snipped flowers from his garden, and one charitable dowager apparently found the means and time to dig up and abscond with a small bush.

It is bad enough that American tourists foul their own nests, but worse, thanks to the creation of cheap jet travel, that our ill-mannered countrymen now commit their nuisances on a worldwide scale. They carve their initials and write their names in lipstick on the walls of the staircase inside St. Peter's Cathedral in Rome. They steal old Bibles from English country churches. Italian police lack courtroom evidence but have every reason to believe that certain American volunteers, helping with the work following the Florence flood, pocketed some of the irreplaceable artifacts they were supposed to be salvaging. A similar brutal egocentrism was displayed by four of our countrymen I found in the Academia in Florence. They were scratching on an early Sienese painting with their fingernails. Asked what the devil they thought they were doing, one of them explained that they were testing the paint.

It must be said that American tourists are not the only ones who do such things—they are merely the worst of the lot. The British contribute their share of those who should know better but act worse, of those like Byron, who carved his initials in a temple, of those like Elgin, who ran away with the marbles. It would seem there is something about tourism itself that brings out the barbarian in any people. The German yields to no one when it comes to oafishness, nor is the Belgian far behind. But American tourists are the worst of all, because they are particularly tactless, tasteless, and loudmouthed, and because there are so many of them and their numbers are increasing.

It is because of tourists' depredations that the great hotels of Europe and America have had to reduce their standards of comfort and elegance to cut their losses. Unmarked cheap napkins, sheets, towels, blankets, glassware, plates, and silverware have replaced the mono-grammed linens, crystal, bone china, and silver of the pre-jet age. If there are still flowers in rooms, they are now apt to be plastic; where there used to be tasteful paintings hanging on the walls of opulent hotel suites, there are now cheap, rather ugly prints in frames screwed into the walls.

The pilfering and vandalism committed by American tourists are not, however, the most repellent of their activities. More obnoxious are the daily outrages they perpetrate against common decency wherever they go. They seem to think that being on vacation implies freedom and irresponsibility, and they express this notion in their dress and behavior. Getting themselves up in lugubrious costumes never worn in their home towns, they invade someone else's home town. Such behavior implies that tourists either think they are alone in the world, or they are ignorant of it.

For example, it seems not to occur to them that a foreign cathedral is a place for worship, not the fun house at an amusement park. I am not a Catholic, but I can certainly sympathize with an French priest who, trying to listen to a confession, also sees and hears a gaggle of irreverent know-nothings clattering and cackling in the Gothic gloom, the bare heads and shoulders of the women an insult to his faith.

I am not a Communist, but I can understand the guards at Lenin's tomb who turned a couple away not because they were Americans, but because the woman was loud, low-bodiced, and miniskirted, while her husband was equally loud-mouthed, and clad in Bermuda shorts, a funny shirt, and a straw hat. Worse, such insensitive egocentrics resent a reprimand.

One young woman jittered in fury on the broad stairs of St. Peter's when refused admission because she was barefoot, wearing only a halter and hot pants. She cursed the nun who barred her way, then stripped off what little she wore, apparently thinking she was thereby making a gesture of righteous protest.

Badgered to despair by such barbarians, the Holy Synod of the Greek Orthodox Church has now asked its monks and nuns to recite, day and night, the following prayer:

"Lord Jesus Christ, Son of God, have mercy on the cities, the islands, and the villages of our Orthodox fatherland . . . which are scourged by the worldly touristic wave. Grace us with a solution of this dramatic problem and protect our brethren who are sorely tried by the modernistic spirit of these contemporary western invaders."

To which, civilized people everywhere can only say "Amen."

Starting Time		Finishing Time	
Reading Time		Reading Rate	
Comprehension		Vocabulary	

Comprehension— Read the following questions and statements. For each one, put an *x* in the box before the option that contains the most complete or accurate answer. Check your answers in the Answer Key on page 107.

1. In the U.S. the expense of protecting public treasures from thoughtless vandals is
   - ☐ a. tax-exempt.
   - ☐ b. unnecessary.
   - ☐ c. lessening.
   - ☐ d. enormous.

2. National parks and memorials are
   - ☐ a. misused by European tourists.
   - ☐ b. used to full advantage.
   - ☐ c. threatened by "nature lovers."
   - ☐ d. abused by all Americans.

3. The Wright brothers' airplane is suspended from the ceiling at the Smithsonian Institute to
   - ☐ a. spare it from vandalism.
   - ☐ b. create a dramatic impact.
   - ☐ c. encourage people to touch it.
   - ☐ d. publicize the damage done by vandals.

4. American tourists would benefit from
   - ☐ a. a lesson in manners.
   - ☐ b. easier access to public monuments.
   - ☐ c. exposure to other cultures.
   - ☐ d. European sensitivities.

5. The Greek Orthodox Church looks upon western influence as
   - ☐ a. a threat to civilized people everywhere.
   - ☐ b. an opportunity to change the modernistic spirit.
   - ☐ c. a solution to a dramatic problem.
   - ☐ d. a threat to its traditions and beliefs.

6. The situation described by the author could be remedied by
   - ☐ a. money and public opinion.
   - ☐ b. improved police surveillance.
   - ☐ c. closing the national parks.
   - ☐ d. education and strict enforcement.

7. The author suggests that vacationing Americans are
   - ☐ a. vulgar and embarrassing.
   - ☐ b. artistic.
   - ☐ c. humble and poor.
   - ☐ d. misunderstood.

8. The selection is meant to be
   - ☐ a. complimentary.
   - ☐ b. humorous.
   - ☐ c. critical.
   - ☐ d. negative.

9. The author considers himself a
   - ☐ a. typical American.
   - ☐ b. civilized person.
   - ☐ c. reformed vandal.
   - ☐ d. sympathetic individual.

10. The author succeeds in making his point by using
    - ☐ a. anger and indignation.
    - ☐ b. restraint and sarcasm.
    - ☐ c. encouragement and flattery.
    - ☐ d. threats and promises.

Comprehension Skills

1. recalling specific facts	6. making a judgment
2. retaining concepts	7. making an inference
3. organizing facts	8. recognizing tone
4. understanding the main idea	9. understanding characters
5. drawing a conclusion	10. appreciation of literary forms

Study Skills, Part One—Following is a passage with blanks where words have been omitted. Next to the passage are groups of five words, one group for each blank. Complete the passage by selecting the correct word for each of the blanks.

The Count-Them Paragraph

   Number six in our discussion of patterns of paragraph development is the Count-Them. This pattern is an inverted development Salestalk—the "pitch" comes first, followed by the facts ___(1)___ it.

(1)   rejecting   supporting
organizing   separating   uniting

Graphically, the Count-Them looks like this:

MAIN IDEA
FACTS
DETAILS
ARGUMENTS

Here is an example of the Count-Them:

College learning deals in abstractions, ideas, principles, laws, theorems, whole movements in history, and so on. This kind of __(2)__ work requires understanding, the perception of relationships, judgment, and reasoning. None of these processes is possible without __(3)__ attention or concentration. Where the mind cannot be held riveted to an idea or principle, understanding __(4)__ or fails completely. Then the necessary connections that must be apprehended are not __(5)__ and the educative process quickly degenerates into rote learning or verbalizing.

In this pattern __(6)__ approach is used. The generalization or main idea is presented first for the reader to see and read. Then the facts and details supporting it are given. This is a pattern used most often in __(7)__ . The author wants the student to see the main point first and then examine the evidence supporting it.

(2) emotional   practical
     theoretical   social   intellectual

(3) occasional   interrupted
     sustained   ordinary   exceptional

(4) hesitates   falters
     continues   perseveres   ceases

(5) pursued   prepared
     perceived   predicted   previewed

(6) innovative   archaic
     formal   casual   obscure

(7) mysteries   novels
     textbooks   plays   essays

Study Skills, Part Two—Read the study skills passage again, paying special attention to the lesson being taught. Then, without looking back at the passage, complete each sentence below by writing in the missing word or words. Check the Answer Key on page 107 for the answers to Study Skills, Part One, and Study Skills, Part Two.

1. The Count-Them paragraph is an inverted _____ .

2. In this kind of paragraph, the main idea is _____ by supporting facts.

3. The main idea in the sample paragraph concerns the abstract nature of _____ learning.

4. This kind of work requires sustained attention or _____ .

5. Textbook authors use this paragraph pattern so that students can see the main idea first and then _____ the evidence supporting it.

12 | # The Day
Man First Flew

Vocabulary—The five words below are from the story you are about to read. Study the words and their meanings. Then complete the ten sentences that follow, using one of the five words to fill in the blank in each sentence. Mark your answer by writing the letter of the word on the line before the sentence. Check your answers in the Answer Key on page 107.

A. epochal: momentous

B. fallacy: false thinking or reasoning

C. compile: gather together

D. erratically: irregularly; unpredictably

E. imprudent: unwise

_____ 1. Orville and Wilbur Wright worked in a wind tunnel to _____ accurate tables of air pressure.

_____ 2. The 12-second flight made on December 17, 1903, was an _____ event.

_____ 3. Although the Wright brothers' plane flew _____ , it *did* fly.

_____ 4. Many people would have thought the Wright brothers _____ for trying to fly into such a strong wind.

_____ 5. Wilbur and Orville Wright began to _____ statistics on air pressure and curved wings in 1901.

_____ 6. Neither Wilbur nor Orville believed their actions at Kitty Hawk were _____ .

_____ 7. The idea that man cannot fly is a _____ .

_____ 8. December 17, 1903 proved to be an _____ day in human history.

_____ 9. Early designs for aircraft were based on the _____ that wings should have a sharp leading edge.

_____ 10. Before the Wright brothers, research in manned flight had been carried out _____ .

At Kitty Hawk, North Carolina, on December 17, 1903, two scientifically minded young men changed the technological complexion of the twentieth century. Resolving the basic problems of flight, Wilbur and Orville Wright piloted a mechanically driven, heavier-than-air machine some 120 feet across a wind-swept stretch of level sand.

Two scientifically minded young men changed the technological complexion of the twentieth century.

That brief first flight lasted no longer than young Johnny Moore might have held his breath while witnessing the epochal event. But the 12 seconds Orville Wright remained aloft were "nevertheless the first in the history of the world in which a machine carrying a man had raised itself by its own power . . . sailed forward without reduction of speed, and finally landed at a point as high as that from which it started."

It meant that thousands of other young aviators would log millions of hours aloft in the half century that followed. Only a few—other than the Wrights themselves—could perceive the results of the unheralded event. Even Wilbur and Orville Wright could hardly imagine that the miracle they had wrought would eventually speed an air-minded generation through aerodynamic barriers and into outer space.

The two persons who were to be the first to fly were born in the Midwest shortly after the Civil War: Wilbur Wright on April 16, 1867, near New Castle, Indiana; Orville Wright on August 19, 1871, in Dayton, Ohio. They were the sons of Milton Wright, a minister of the United Brethren Church. As boys they shared a common interest in mechanical devices. When they first began to think of trying to fly, they were operating the Wright Cycle Company in Dayton, manufacturing, selling, and repairing bicycles.

Always interested in science, they were much impressed by the gliding experiments in Germany of Otto Lilienthal, the father of gliding and the first to explain scientifically why curved surfaces in a flying machine are superior to flat surfaces. The Wrights always considered Lilienthal their greatest inspiration.

They believed that a glider should be built in such a way that the right and left wings could be presented at different angles to the wind for sidewise balance, and they determined to do this by warping or twisting the wings. To try their scheme for control, they built a five-foot model of a glider and, one day in 1899, tested it. Then they started thinking of a place for testing a man-carrying glider. After a study of wind records obtained from the Weather Bureau at Washington, they picked Kitty Hawk. During their first stay there in September, 1900, they camped in a tent. Returning the next year with a larger glider, they built a camp a few hundred feet north of Kill

Devil Hill. In their gliding experiments of 1900 and 1901 they got less lifting power from the wings than existing tables of air pressures on curved surfaces had led them to expect. This caused them to believe that all of these tables must be wrong.

After their return to Dayton, experiments led them to new knowledge about wing design. In a small wind tunnel, they tested more than 200 types of miniature wing surfaces. Among other things, these experiments proved the fallacy of a sharp leading edge of an airplane wing and the inefficiency of deeply cambered wings, then generally advocated.

In a few weeks they accomplished work of almost incalculable importance. Not only were they the first to test miniature wings accurately, they were the first in the world to compile tables of figures from which one might design an airplane that could fly. The Wright brothers' wind-tunnel experiments marked a turning point in the efforts of man to conquer the air.

The brothers returned to Kill Devil Hill in 1902 with a glider having a wingspan of 32 feet, built according to their own figures on wind pressure.

It was soon evident that this 1902 glider showed a great advance over any other ever built. In it, they made many glides of more than 600 feet against a 36-mile-an-hour wind. No previous experimenter had ever dared try to glide in so stiff a wind.

With the 1902 glider the Wrights solved the major problems of equilibrium; now they felt sure they could build a successful power machine.

The next year they built both *The Flyer,* a craft with a wingspan of more than 40 feet, and the powerplant, a 12-horsepower engine, weighing 200 pounds. Its two propellers, designed according to their own calculations, were the first predictable-performance propellers ever built. Machine and pilot together weighed about 750 pounds.

It was late in September 1903 when the Wrights reached their camp at Kill Devil Hill. Delayed by mechanical problems and bad weather, they were not ready until December 14 to fly their machine. The first trial was not quite successful. Without enough wind to start from level ground, they took the machine to the slope of the hill where they placed the sledlike skids on a "truck"—a plank about 6 feet long, with rollers—which rested on a monorail track. Wilbur won the toss of a coin for what he called the "first whack." When *The Flyer* left the track and before it had gained enough speed, Wilbur turned it upward too suddenly. It climbed a few feet, stalled, and settled to the ground near the foot of the hill after being in the air just 3½ seconds. One of the skids and several other parts were broken. Two days were needed for making repairs.

On the morning of December 17, the wind blew at 22 to 27 miles an hour. Hoping it would die down, the Wrights waited. When it continued, they decided to go ahead and attempt a flight. On a smooth stretch of level ground just west of their camp, they laid a 60-foot track, pointing directly into the wind. (The takeoff spot is now marked by a granite boulder.)

By the time all was ready, three men from the Kill Devil Hill Lifesaving Station and two others had arrived.

It was now Orville's turn. Before climbing aboard the machine, he put his camera on a tripod and asked John T. Daniels of the United States Lifesaving Crew to press the button when the machine had risen directly in front of the camera. Nestled in the control mechanism on the lower wing, Orville started the machine down the track, traveling slowly into a 27-mile-an-hour headwind. After running 40 feet on the track, the plane took off, climbed about 10 feet in the air, darted erratically up and down several times, and dipped suddenly to earth about 120 feet from takeoff point.

As Orville Wright put it: "This flight lasted only 12 seconds, but it was nevertheless the first in history in which a machine carrying a man had raised itself by its own power into the air in full flight, had sailed forward without reduction of speed, and finally landed at a point as high as that from which it started."

The brothers alternated in making three more flights that morning, each longer than the previous one; on the fourth flight, Wilbur flew 852 feet in 59 seconds.

As it seemed imprudent to fly at much height at first, it was sometimes impossible to correct the up and down motion of the machine before it struck the ground. This accounts for the flights being so short. While the Wrights and onlookers were discussing the flights, a gust of wind struck the plane and rolled it over, damaging it badly. It could not be repaired in time for any more flights that year; in fact, it never flew again.

In 1928 Orville Wright (Wilbur had died in 1912) lent the plane to the Science Museum at South Kensington, England, with the understanding that it would remain there until he requested its return. In 1942 he asked the museum to send the plane back to the United States after World War II. After Orville's death in 1948, his executors deposited the plane in the National Air Museum of the Smithsonian Institution, where it was formally placed on exhibition on December 17, 1948, the 45th anniversary of the first flights.

Starting Time		Finishing Time	
Reading Time		Reading Rate	
Comprehension		Vocabulary	

Comprehension — Read the following questions and statements. For each one, put an x in the box before the option that contains the most complete or accurate answer. Check your answers in the Answer Key on page 107.

1. The 1902 glider
   - ☐ a. uncovered serious mechanical problems.
   - ☐ b. embarrassed Otto Lilienthal.
   - ☐ c. discouraged the Wright brothers.
   - ☐ d. solved major problems of equilibrium.

2. The significance of the Wright brothers' "miracle" was appreciated by
   - ☐ a. the federal government.
   - ☐ b. the space agency.
   - ☐ c. very few people.
   - ☐ d. the general public.

3. The Wrights became fans of Otto Lilienthal
   - ☐ a. after their 1903 flight.
   - ☐ b. during experimentation with wing design.
   - ☐ c. while running a bicycle shop.
   - ☐ d. during their first glider trial at Kill Devil Hill.

4. The purpose of the selection is to
   - ☐ a. immortalize the Wright brothers.
   - ☐ b. demonstrate American ingenuity.
   - ☐ c. describe the beginning of aviation.
   - ☐ d. develop enthusiasm for flying.

5. *The Flyer* was unusual because it was
   - ☐ a. self-propelled.
   - ☐ b. man-operated.
   - ☐ c. instantly popular.
   - ☐ d. surprisingly fast.

6. One of the basic problems of flight in 1902 was to
   - ☐ a. find the proper fuel mixture.
   - ☐ b. find a proper landing field.
   - ☐ c. attract sufficient financial backing.
   - ☐ d. make a flying machine that was heavier than air.

7. The failure of *The Flyer* to perform on its maiden flight was most probably due to
   ☐ a. a sudden gust of wind.
   ☐ b. an error of judgment.
   ☐ c. a defective fuel pump.
   ☐ d. a mechanical failure.

8. The tone of Orville Wright's statement about his 12-second flight is
   ☐ a. skeptical.   ☐ c. elated.
   ☐ b. dogmatic.   ☐ d. brave.

9. The Wright brothers' method of investigation revealed their
   ☐ a. basic insecurity.
   ☐ b. independent minds.
   ☐ c. fear of the unknown.
   ☐ d. disregard for public opinion.

10. The selection is written in the form of
    ☐ a. a narrative.
    ☐ b. an essay.
    ☐ c. a biography.
    ☐ d. an autobiography.

Comprehension Skills

1. recalling specific facts	6. making a judgment
2. retaining concepts	7. making an inference
3. organizing facts	8. recognizing tone
4. understanding the main idea	9. understanding characters
5. drawing a conclusion	10. appreciation of literary forms

Study Skills, Part One—Following is a passage with blanks where words have been omitted. Next to the passage are groups of five words, one group for each blank. Complete the passage by selecting the correct word for each of the blanks.

The Because Paragraph

The Because pattern of paragraph development is the same as the Therefore, turned upside down. The conclusion or generalization is presented first, followed by the ___(1)___ arguments leading to it.

Graphically the Because looks like this:

MAIN IDEA
ARGUMENTS
IN
SUPPORT
OF

Here is an example of the Because:

Concentration, then, ___(2)___ your consciousness to some object and heightens your awareness of that object. There are a thousand things that might enter consciousness if you let them. The fact is you allow only a few things into your ___(3)___ at any one time. Those things, moreover, are in some way bound up with your ___(4)___ , needs, hopes, interests, and purposes. Thus concentration functions something like a spotlight. It highlights things that are of ___(5)___ to you so that they stand out in sharp

(1)   concentrated   sequential
      scattered   alternating   forceful

(2)   expands   broadens
      narrows   subjects   obscures

(3)   consciousness   environment
      surroundings   emotions   thoughts

(4)   dislikes   temptations
      dreams   potentials   wants

(5)   irritation   significance
      delight   puzzlement   inconsequence

relief. At the same time, it throws into ___(6)___ (i.e., to the background of consciousness) items of experience that are not of particular interest or importance at the moment.

(6)   disorder   light
       shadow   confusion   focus

The Because paragraph and its opposite, the Therefore, are used in the same way by the student: find and read the conclusion first; then read and ___(7)___ the steps leading to it.

(7)   discount   avoid
      evaluate   forget   accept

Study Skills, Part Two—Read the study skills passage again, paying special attention to the lesson being taught. Then, without looking back at the passage, complete each sentence below by writing in the missing word or words. Check the Answer Key on page 107 for the answers to Study Skills, Part One, and Study Skills, Part Two.

1. The Because paragraph is the _____ paragraph turned upside down.

2. The main idea is followed by sequential _____ .

3. In the sample paragraph, the main idea states that concentration heightens your _____ of an object.

4. The function of concentration is compared to that of a _____ .

5. The Because paragraph and its _____ , the Therefore paragraph, are used by the student in the same way.

13 | Preserving Alaska's Prehistory

by Downs Matthews

Vocabulary—The five words below are from the story you are about to read. Study the words and their meanings. Then complete the ten sentences that follow, using one of the five words to fill in the blank in each sentence. Mark your answer by writing the letter of the word on the line before the sentence. Check your answers in the Answer Key on page 107.

A. consortium: association; partnership

B. initiated: began

C. ensuing: following

D. sully: spoil

E. contends: asserts; states firmly

_____ 1. Alyeska _____ work on the pipeline only after archaeologists surveyed the route.

_____ 2. The _____ which is responsible for building the pipeline is the Alyeska Pipeline Service Company.

_____ 3. Neither pipeline workers nor archaeologists wanted to _____ important archaeological sites.

_____ 4. In the _____ years, we will have much greater knowledge of prehistoric Alaskan societies.

_____ 5. The curator of the Alaskan State Museum _____ that the construction of the pipeline affords Alaskans a great opportunity.

_____ 6. The _____ took great care to preserve the remains of ancient Alaskan cultures.

_____ 7. Jim Corbin _____ that Eskimos and Athapaskans often bartered for goods.

_____ 8. The author does not address the question of whether the pipeline will _____ Alaska's natural beauty.

_____ 9. No one knows who first _____ the bartering between different Alaskan cultures.

_____ 10. _____ generations may wonder what Alaska looked like before the pipeline was built.

From a knoll above the south bank of the Atigun River you can see for miles up the broad caribou trail that winds along the valley floor. Across the icy stream, a cow moose browses lazily. Along a high ridge of jagged blond rock—a finger jutting from the vast Brooks Range that sprawls whitely to the south—a herd of mountain

Digs along the Alaskan pipeline route are producing evidence of early mankind in America.

sheep files daintily toward an alpine meadow. To the north, Galbraith Lake sparkles amid the descending foothills of Alaska's North Slope, its surface dotted with southbound ducks.

For the tiny community of Nunamiut Eskimos that settled here, it was a great place to camp. Well-drained, protected from wind, close to wood and water, it straddled the migration routes of the great game herds which were food and clothing to the Inland Eskimo peoples. Here, they could live and prosper.

"Several families settled here about a hundred years ago," explains archaeologist Jim Corbin, whose analysis of the site will earn him a Ph.D. from Washington State University. "Their name for the place was Aniganigurak. The outside world didn't find them until 1950, when a bush pilot landed here."

Today, Aniganigurak lives only in the memories of a few aged Eskimos who remember visiting there as children. But its contribution to our understanding of Alaska's prehistory is now secure, thanks to archaeological surveys being conducted under the direction of Dr. John Cook, of the University of Alaska, and Professor William Workman, of Alaska Methodist University, with the cooperation of the Arctic Institute of North America. Their angel: Alyeska Pipeline Service Company, a consortium of firms formed to build an 800-mile pipeline from the Prudhoe Bay oilfields to the port of Valdez in southern Alaska. Alyeska initiated the surveys in 1969 to assure that whatever archaeological information the pipeline might turn up along its right-of-way would be properly preserved and analyzed.

"Construction activities sometimes destroy valuable archaeological sites that might have shed some important light on our prehistoric heritage," says Dr. Cook. "But the trans-Alaska pipeline is an extraordinary story of exactly the opposite situation."

The 800-mile traverse of the entire state is regarded by archaeologists and anthropologists as the opportunity of a lifetime. Michael Kennedy, curator of the Alaska State Museum in Juneau and a member of the state's Antiquities Commission, believes the project has already contributed knowledge of "inestimable value to Alaska. No state has ever before had the opportunity to cut a transection from one end to the other to examine the development of man's society and culture there," Kennedy

points out. "We're tremendously excited about it."

What the archaeologists may learn in Alaska may answer questions about the early inhabitants of both North and South America. "The original human inhabitants of the New World migrated from Asia across a land bridge that is now the Bering Strait," explains Dr. Cook. They came 50,000 to 60,000 years ago—small tribes of nomads following herds of bison, horse, and mammoth. For thousands of years, while this migration was taking place, Alaska was a major occupation zone. "But, actually," Cook says, "we have little solid evidence of these early hunters. The pipeline will pass through parts of the state where they must have lived, and it is highly probable that it will uncover some of their campsites. We plan to have people watching closely throughout the entire construction phase."

Cook believes information uncovered by the pipeline may also explain what effect changes in Alaska's environment may have had during ensuing centuries on the culture and physiology of the descendants of these first immigrants. "What these changes were and how they came about may help mankind everywhere understand the process of change and adaptation of human populations," he observes.

In 1970, with the pipeline still in the planning stage, archaeologists began walking the entire route in search of sites. Working out of Alyeska base camps, field parties boarded company helicopters each day to be airlifted to and from points along the line. In this way, they were able to cover lots of ground. "We did in two summers what normally would have taken four or five years," Cook says.

Alyeska personnel took a great interest in the work, Cook reports. "They couldn't have been more cooperative," he says. "They showed movies on archaeology and encouraged the men to report anything of interest to us. We got lots of tips."

Elsewhere in the state, company geologists and other exploration personnel have discovered and reported archaeological sites. One was excavated during the summers of 1967–1970 under the direction of Professor Edwin S. Hall, of Ohio State University. It yielded particularly important information on a critical period in Eskimo culture—a time when Eskimos were evolving from the stone age, and making their transition from a self-sustaining society into one depending on goods of outside manufacture. In his report on the dig, Professor Hall praised the care taken by crews not to sully the area. "They left no sign of their passing here," he wrote.

Locating a site along the pipeline route, a field party would map and excavate it immediately. As most were small prehistoric campsites, the work could be completed quickly. Few sites were found along the southern portion of the route, chiefly because of the presence of heavy undergrowth. "We still have almost everything to learn about the prehistory of this area," Professor Workman says, "but I suspect that when the evidence begins to come in, we'll find that this rich and beautiful country has supported a relatively large population for some thousands of years, just as it did in late prehistoric times."

Along the more barren northern half of the line, 189 sites were found and excavated. Altogether, they yielded more than 8,500 items of archaeological significance ranging in age from recent times to more than 13,000 years. All but two were the remains of hunting camps once used by small groups of men in their seasonal pursuit of migrating caribou and other game. The digs produced no tools used typically by women, such as thimbles or small knives called ulus. Of the two permanent settlements, only one, the Atigun Canyon site of Antiganigurak, lay directly in the pipeline's path. Because of its importance, Corbin devoted a full summer to its careful excavation.

Corbin indicates the outlines of seven moss houses that once stood here. (Igloos were unheard of in Alaska, he says.) "To build a moss house, they would erect a framework of willow poles and pile a foot-thick layer of ground moss on top of it as insulation," he explains. Inside, the Eskimo family would weave a floor mat of willow branches. Over this they would spread furs for rugs and bedding. In the center under a smokehole in the roof, they constructed a stone hearth. Outside, other flat stones served as workbenches on which to make tools or prepare meat for cooking.

Corbin thinks his long-vanished friends came to the site between 1870 and 1880. "Many Eskimos fled to remote places during that period to escape diseases that ravaged much of Alaska's population at that time," he explains. "They lived off the land as their ancestors had lived for centuries." He exhibits stone knives and arrow points, needles and thimbles of ivory, a shovel fashioned of caribou antler, fishing gear of bone and wood. But also trade goods: blue china beads from England and brass cartridge cases for a .44 Henry and a .45 Colt. "The Eskimo and Atha-paskan peoples bartered widely for such items," Corbin says. "They got them from their southern relatives who swapped with Canadian and English fur traders."

Although Aniganigurak isn't old as archaeological sites go, Corbin feels it offers a rare challenge to his science. "This is one of the few spots in the world where we can analyze a site using the techniques of modern archaeology, and then check our findings for accuracy against the recollections of living men who remember how it was," he says. "If our methods give us wrong answers here, they could be misleading us elsewhere. And if this is true, how can we assure greater reliability?"

Although complete analysis of data gained from the Alyeska surveys is several years away, a general picture is emerging of how the prehistoric Eskimo survived in a hostile climate and rugged land. "The sites reflect a nomadic seasonal hunting pattern," Cook says. "The woman and children stayed at home while the men searched for game." The grouping of their campsites in certain areas suggests that they found hunting more profitable where the presence of several different types of terrain and ground cover provided a variety of animal life. "For example, we have found camps grouped along the sea coast, in the northern foothills of the Brooks Range, and in the hill and river area of the Yukon-Tanana Upland," Cook points out. "If the caribou failed to show up, they could always go fishing, or try for sheep or moose."

On the other hand, in the barren ground well north of the Brooks Range, and on the Range's southern flanks, field parties found few camps. "Hunting in these areas would have been confined to only one type of game," Cook explains. "If the hunter's luck was poor, he had nothing else to turn to, so he couldn't risk going there."

Early analysis also suggests that the boundaries between the Eskimo and Athapaskan Indian cultures shifted back and forth many times over the centuries. "It's probable that each society contacted and learned from the other," Cook believes. "We're learning a lot about regional variations and transitions in their cultures through archaeological time."

An equally important result of the project, Cook contends, is the precedent set by Alyeska in northern archaeology. "If a commercial organization can show the concern, cooperation, and communication to effect a project of this magnitude, then it will be difficult for others to ignore the Federal Antiquities Act," he believes. "It's the start of a new era for archaeology up here."

The Alaskan pipeline was completed in 1977. The project cost about $8 billion.

Starting Time		Finishing Time	
Reading Time		Reading Rate	
Comprehension		Vocabulary	

Comprehension— Read the following questions and statements. For each one, put an *x* in the box before the option that contains the most complete or accurate answer. Check your answers in the Answer Key on page 107.

1. The archaeological digs conducted along the Alaskan pipeline route produced no
   - ☐ a. evidence of early hunters.
   - ☐ b. household tools used by women.
   - ☐ c. remains of dwellings.
   - ☐ d. recognizable weapons.

2. Aniganigurak
   - ☐ a. became overrun by some hostile northern tribes.
   - ☐ b. supplied all the needs of its early settlers.
   - ☐ c. figured prominently in the development of Alaska.
   - ☐ d. offers poor prospects for any permanent habitations.

3. Aleyska agreed to the archaeological digs
   - ☐ a. after much coaxing by archaeologists.
   - ☐ b. when the Alaskan government became involved.
   - ☐ c. at the very beginning of the project.
   - ☐ d. after a huge public outcry.

4. This selection demonstrates that
   - ☐ a. the environment must be protected from man's destructiveness.
   - ☐ b. the pattern of civilization has changed tremendously over the last few centuries.
   - ☐ c. society can benefit from industry in unusual ways.
   - ☐ d. archaeologists must use creative methods to investigate the past.

5. The information uncovered by the pipeline may help predict the
   - ☐ a. energy requirements of America in the year 2000.
   - ☐ b. effects of present environmental changes on future populations.
   - ☐ c. the rate of population growth in isolated communities.
   - ☐ d. migration movements of wild herds.

6. The interest shown by the Alaska Pipeline Service Company in Alaska's prehistory is encouraging and should
   - ☐ a. increase government financing.
   - ☐ b. reduce construction costs.
   - ☐ c. enhance its public image.
   - ☐ d. determine Alaska's future.

7. Archaeology concerns itself with
   - ☐ a. construction pipelines.
   - ☐ b. Alaska's development.
   - ☐ c. ancient civilizations.
   - ☐ d. threatened ecology.

8. The selection ends on a note of
   - ☐ a. warning. ☐ c. entreaty.
   - ☐ b. despair. ☐ d. optimism.

9. Jim Corbin
   - ☐ a. prides himself on his past accomplishments.
   - ☐ b. is disgusted by Alyeska's actions.
   - ☐ c. cares deeply about Alaska's past.
   - ☐ d. fears for Alaska's future.

10. The description of a jagged rock as "a finger jutting from the vast Brooks Range" is an example of
    - ☐ a. personification. ☐ c. an allusion.
    - ☐ b. a metaphor. ☐ d. a simile.

Comprehension Skills	
1. recalling specific facts	6. making a judgment
2. retaining concepts	7. making an inference
3. organizing facts	8. recognizing tone
4. understanding the main idea	9. understanding characters
5. drawing a conclusion	10. appreciation of literary forms

Study Skills, Part One—Following is a passage with blanks where words have been omitted. Next to the passage are groups of five words, one group for each blank. Complete the passage by selecting the correct word for each of the blanks.

The Come-On Paragraph

This pattern of paragraph development is different from ___(1)___ we have already seen in that the main idea comes at neither the beginning nor the end; it comes in the middle.

(1) some   those
  many none several

This pattern leads the reader into the paragraph first and then presents the main idea. This is usually followed by ___(2)___ thoughts pertaining to the generalizations. Graphically, the Come-On looks like this:

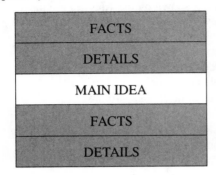

FACTS

DETAILS

MAIN IDEA

FACTS

DETAILS

Here is an example of the Come-On:

Every scholar is plagued with the problem of ___(3)___ (it is really counter-attraction) during study. What should be done about it? Well, one good practical rule is to be on the alert for the first ___(4)___ of your concentration. You can then nip wool-gathering in the bud. If you try to understand each thought as the author presents it, there is little ___(5)___ that your mind will wander. Reading an abstruse passage without understanding it breaks the ___(6)___ of your thought. There is then a tendency to substitute your own fancies for the author's ideas.

This pattern makes for interesting reading. The introductory ideas ___(7)___ the reader and lead him into the paragraph. Then the author lets the reader see the main idea and some additional facts relating to it.

(2)   obscure   helpful
    additional   distracting   confusing

(3)   concentration   involvement
    procrastination   substitution   distraction

(4)   failure   wavering
    heightening   improvement   perfection

(5)   danger   thought
    hope   belief   proof

(6)   sequence   dispersion
    disposal   continuity   commitment

(7)   entice   disgust
    distract   entertain   discourage

Study Skills, Part Two—Read the study skills passage again, paying special attention to the lesson being taught. Then, without looking back at the passage, complete each sentence below by writing in the missing word or words. Check the Answer Key on page 107 for the answers to Study Skills, Part One, and Study Skills, Part Two.

1. The Come-On paragraph is different from the others because the main idea is

   in the _____ .

2. The main idea is followed by additional _____ that pertain to it.

3. In the sample paragraph, the main idea states that good concentration can be

   sustained by understanding each thought as it is _____ .

4. If you try to read a difficult passage without _____ it, your attention

   may waver.

5. This paragraph pattern entices the reader with interesting _____ ideas.

14 | Hiroshima— Death and Rebirth, I

by C. E. Maine

Vocabulary—The five words below are from the story you are about to read. Study the words and their meanings. Then complete the ten sentences that follow, using one of the five words to fill in the blank in each sentence. Mark your answer by writing the letter of the word on the line before the sentence. Check your answers in the Answer Key on page 108.

A. capitulated: surrendered

B. discernible: detectable

C. remote: far away; removed

D. intolerably: unbearably

E. typical: representative

_____ 1. Radioactivity is not _____ with the naked eye.

_____ 2. Many people with severe injuries found themselves _____ thirsty.

_____ 3. Yoshio was lucky to be in a fairly _____ part of the city when the bomb exploded.

_____ 4. The deadly effects of the bomb were immediately _____ throughout the shattered city.

_____ 5. The residents of Hiroshima were _____ Japanese citizens.

_____ 6. The people of Hiroshima had been warned that unless Japan _____ their city would be bombed.

_____ 7. The desire to get to the hospital was a reaction _____ of the survivors.

_____ 8. If Japan had _____ sooner, America would not have dropped the atomic bomb.

_____ 9. Many people injured in the blast found their burns and wounds _____ painful.

_____ 10. People in a _____ section of the city had a better chance of surviving the blast than did people at the epicenter of the explosion.

On August 6, 1945, Hiroshima literally exploded and burned itself into the pages of human history.

Near the southwestern tip of Honshu, the largest of the four main islands that make up the boomerang shape of Japan, lies the sizeable industrial city of Hiroshima. Until the closing days of the Second World War comparatively few people in the West had ever heard of the place, and then suddenly, on 6 August, 1945, Hiroshima literally exploded and burned itself immortally into the pages of human history. The world has never been the same since.

At about seven o'clock on that particular morning in the late summer of 1945 the air-raid sirens wailed throughout Hiroshima. Young Yoshio, hurrying on his daily newspaper delivery round, was unconcerned; nearly every morning American high-flying planes would pass over on reconnaissance missions, but there had been no bombs. The city had been surprisingly free from air attack, even though its harbor, oil refineries, factories, arsenal, and garrison of some 150,000 troops made it a legitimate military target.

To Yoshio and many of his fellow citizens the explanation was simple enough. Hiroshima had been spared because so many local inhabitants had emigrated to America before the war and had managed to persuade the United States political hierarchy to overlook the city— and it was even rumored that a distant relative of President Truman was living anonymously in the neighborhood. On the other hand, ten days earlier an American plane had dropped leaflets on the town warning that it would be among the Japanese cities to be destroyed by air attack unless Japan capitulated immediately. There was no discernable alarm, but then the leaflets had not mentioned that the air attack when it came would consist of one single bomb that had cost millions to develop and was destined to change the course of history.

The local authorities were taking the usual precautions. Later in the day, when his job was finished, fifteen-year-old Yoshio would be joining other youths and students in demolishing houses and other property—much of it constructed from wood—to create fire-breaks in the event of bombing. It was all rather fun and somewhat remote from reality.

The population of Hiroshima at that time numbered around 343,000. Although many people and children had been evacuated from the city, there remained about a quarter of a million in the business and residential center which covered an area of four square miles. It was in that central zone that Yoshio lived in a small house with his parents. In an hour or so, when his work was finished, he would be returning home for a late breakfast with his mother; by then his father would already have left for work in the factory.

As usual, the air-raid alert proved uneventful and the all-clear was sounded soon after seven-thirty. Very few people had bothered to take cover in air-raid shelters. At eight o'clock a radio news bulletin mentioned that two or three American B29 Super-Fortresses had been sighted, but they were flying high at around 30,000 feet and were obviously reconnaissance planes. In fact, as the casual and reassuring news announcement was being made, the bombardier in the B29 Super-Fortress *Enola Gay,* commanded by Colonel Paul W. Tibbets of the United States Army Air Force, had already released the first atomic bomb ever to be used in warfare. From a height of five miles it parachuted down with deadly precision to the center of Hiroshima. At a predetermined altitude of 1,500 feet two slugs of plutonium inside the bomb fused together to form an over-critical mass—the chain reaction of nuclear fission was instant, incandescent, and incredibly violent. That one bomb released the destructive impact of 20,000 tons of TNT.

All that Yoshio could afterwards remember of that significant moment of history was the blinding white flash in the morning sky and the intolerably searing heat. He was lucky, for he was two miles from the epicenter of the explosion and close to a friend's house. Nevertheless for a few moments he lost consciousness in the heat-flash and blast, and recovered to find himself crumpled against a tottering wall and the air full of flying debris.

Confused and afraid, he dragged himself to his feet and hurried to his friend's house. Only the walls remained standing—the roof, windows, and doors had been torn violently away as if by a giant unseen hand. Stumbling into the ruins of the house, Yoshio came almost immediately upon the dead body of his friend, broken among the rubble and skewered by a long shard of glass. He stood for a while, stunned and unable to think, and gradually became aware of his own wounds, but they seemed slight enough—some cuts and abrasions and a painfully bruised shoulder.

His mind still blank and uncomprehending, he went out into the road again. An incredible mass of dark cloud was rising swiftly above the center of the city and spreading outwards at its summit to form a gigantic mushroom. Beneath it other clouds boiled and unfolded in turbulent motion. Across the city whirlwinds sucked dust and debris into the darkening air. Now there was a new light in the sky—a flickering orange glow from thousands of burning buildings adding their own smoke to the expanding mushroom.

From the wreckage screams and groans came from all directions, but Yoshio had no ears for them. Only one thing mattered at that moment—to return home as quickly as possible and find his parents. He ran desperately, stumbling and gasping in the foul air, making for the city center where he lived, but soon had to stop in total bewilderment. Before him was a vast wilderness of smouldering ruins. There was no way of finding the street, let alone the house, where he had lived all his life. Almost every building had been razed to the ground, and it was only by the surviving metal ribs of the dome of what had been the Museum of Science and Industry that he was able to gain a sense of direction.

For a long time he wandered around, seeking some recognizable landmarks of his own familiar neighborhood, but in vain. It was dangerous to stay any longer. The fires were spreading and in places the ground was so hot that it burned his shoes; very soon the center of the city would be a raging inferno.

Reluctantly he abandoned his quest. Saying a short prayer for his mother and father and silently promising them that he would return, he made his way toward the suburbs, the river, and safety. Now he responded to screams and cries from the ruins around him and helped others to dig among the rubble, but the fire spread so quickly that the rescuers were forced to leave the trapped victims to be suffocated or burned alive.

He became aware of horrors around him which he had ignored in the obsessive search for his parents. Men, women, and children, their bodies grotesquely burned by the heatflash of the bomb, dragged themselves painfully away from the fires that threatened to overtake them. Some, whose faces must have been turned toward the flash, no longer had recognizable features, and their unprotected hands were charred claws. Many had found their way to water tanks to immerse their heads and ease the pain—only to die where they lay.

The refugees from the stricken city grew quickly in number. They did not talk nor, outside of family groups, did they help each other. Yoshio found himself one of this strange, stumbling procession of automatons.

Suddenly he heard his name called. He turned and recognized the girl running toward him as his cousin. Her face was scarlet with burns, and her hair and clothes had been severely scorched. He took off his shirt to cover her and observed that the gaily flowered pattern of her kimono had duplicated itself on her body where the heat-flash had penetrated the darker colors and been partly reflected by the lighter ones.

Her story was typical of many. She had been on her way to school when the flash came and the world collapsed around her. For a while she had been totally blinded, but when she could see again the fires had prevented her from trying to return home, so she had simply joined the stream of refugees, too shocked to think for herself. She had no idea what had become of her parents, who were Yoshio's uncle and aunt.

Yoshio decided to get her to a hospital for urgent treatment, overlooking the fact that there were thousands of others aiming for the same destination. In fact, so dense was the crowd of injured people surrounding the hospital that it was impossible to push a way through. He did know that only three of Hiroshima's hospitals were left standing, while most of the doctors and nurses were dead or too seriously wounded to be able to work. Those who remained worked unceasingly day and night with inadequate facilities and supplies until suitable help could be obtained from nearby towns.

Yoshio and his cousin decided to go to a park on the river bank where at least there would be water and shade. Here the grass was still green and relatively unscorched, for it was quite a long way from the epicenter of the explosion. Then came the rain—black and viscous like oil—but it did not last long enough to damp down the flames of the burning city. It was merely precipitation of the hot air from the explosion as it rose and condensed over the city, but it brought down with it the radioactive dust of destruction.

There were thousands in the park, but Yoshio and the girl found a place near the river where she could lie down to rest. Hunting around the riverbank he found a small chipped pot which he filled with water to take back to his cousin. The girl sipped a little with difficulty through her scorched lips and then vomited, but presently she drank some more and seemed easier. He left her in a quiet sleep.

The water incident had not gone unnoticed. All around him, heat-flash victims were asking for water, and for an hour or two Yoshio acted as a water-carrier for those too ill to help themselves. The service ended suddenly when an official knocked the chipped pot from his hand so that it shattered on the ground. Yoshio's angry outburst was silenced when the official explained that water was extremely harmful for people with those kinds of injuries.

Early in the afternoon the fire reached the park, but here it was easier to control and a chain of men succeeded in holding the flames at bay—though not before the panic-stricken crowds had pressed toward the comparative safety in such numbers that many of the weaker ones were drowned. Some managed to reach the sandbanks in the middle of the river where they thought they were safe— and so they were, until the tide rose and swept them away. In the park itself the living, the dying, and the dead lay side by side. People died quietly, without making a sound.

Starting Time		Finishing Time	
Reading Time		Reading Rate	
Comprehension		Vocabulary	

Comprehension— Read the following questions and statements. For each one, put an *x* in the box before the option that contains the most complete or accurate answer. Check your answers in the Answer Key on page 108.

1. Hiroshima was
   - ☐ a. a secondary military target.
   - ☐ b. the former capital of Japan.
   - ☐ c. the center of Japanese power.
   - ☐ d. a legitimate military target.

2. The cumulative impact of what he saw and heard left Yoshio
   - ☐ a. with uncontrollable hatred.
   - ☐ b. with resigned acceptance.
   - ☐ c. in a hopeful condition.
   - ☐ d. in a state of shock.

3. Yoshio gave up his quest to find his parents' home
   - ☐ a. after finding his injured cousin.
   - ☐ b. when fires spread through the city.
   - ☐ c. when he found the body of his dead friend.
   - ☐ d. just as a black, viscous rain began to fall.

4. The purpose of the selection is to
   - ☐ a. condemn American policy.
   - ☐ b. expose Japanese duplicity.
   - ☐ c. portray the horror of war.
   - ☐ d. create sympathy for Yoshio.

5. The world has never been the same since August 6, 1945, because
   - ☐ a. Hiroshima demonstrated the destructiveness of atomic power.
   - ☐ b. Japan afterwards became a major industrial power.
   - ☐ c. World War II was brought to a conclusion.
   - ☐ d. the U.S. imprisoned thousands of Japanese sympathizers.

6. The reasons given by some of the people to explain why Hiroshima had been free from air attacks were an example of
   - ☐ a. self-deception.
   - ☐ b. military analysis.
   - ☐ c. political awareness.
   - ☐ d. disguised cowardice.

7. The official reaction to the warning leaflets suggests which of the following?
   - ☐ a. The city was impregnable to air attack.
   - ☐ b. The United States would not dare destroy Hiroshima.
   - ☐ c. The Japanese were not expecting an atomic attack.
   - ☐ d. The population had been secretly evacuated the week before.

8. The description of the aftermath of the explosion elicits feelings of
   - ☐ a. admiration.
   - ☐ b. awe and fear.
   - ☐ c. hope.
   - ☐ d. surprise and curiosity.

9. Yoshio was
   - ☐ a. an ungrateful child.
   - ☐ b. a devoted son.
   - ☐ c. a selfish individual.
   - ☐ d. an heroic person.

10. The statement "Her face was scarlet with burns" is an example of
    - ☐ a. hyperbole.
    - ☐ b. literal language.
    - ☐ c. a simile.
    - ☐ d. a metaphor.

Comprehension Skills

1. recalling specific facts	6. making a judgment
2. retaining concepts	7. making an inference
3. organizing facts	8. recognizing tone
4. understanding the main idea	9. understanding characters
5. drawing a conclusion	10. appreciation of literary forms

Study Skills, Part One—Following is a passage with blanks where words have been omitted. Next to the passage are groups of five words, one group for each blank. Complete the passage by selecting the correct word for each of the blanks.

The Switch Paragraph

   This pattern of paragraph development is also different from the ___(1)___ in that its main idea, too, comes at neither end but in the middle.

(1)   proceeding   following
       others   first   last

Graphically, the Switch looks like this:

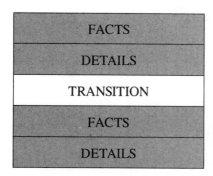

FACTS
DETAILS
TRANSITION
FACTS
DETAILS

Here is an example of the Switch:

In other instances the automobile at college is
a pure luxury. Under this ___(2)___ would fall: short
hops to beaneries, taverns, and other nearby resorts;
long jaunts to root the team on, travel for the sheer
joy of keeping on the move, and driving for the sake
of dating. All these ___(3)___ help to make college
life worth living, but they do eat into a student's
time; and they also eat into his ___(4)___ . Of course,
a parent is sometimes persuaded that a car is one
of those uncatalogued but ___(5)___ expenses of higher
education; and so the parent unwittingly contributes
to the student's academic delinquency. At other times
it is not unheard of for a student to be so smitten
with a(n) ___(6)___ for the social prestige conferred
by the possession of a car that he will take a part-
time job in order to pay for its upkeep.

Notice how this example of the Switch is effectively
used to discuss the pros and cons of having an ___(7)___
on campus. The writer's main idea statement is used to
make the transition from one side to the other.

(2)   argument   discussion
       heading   detail   opinion

(3)   dreams   disappointments
       pleasures   challenges   intentions

(4)   ego   pocketbook
       confidence   leisure   work

(5)   unnecessary   necessary
       unexpected   planned   welcome

(6)   dislike   fear
       inclination   desire   distaste

(7)   aggressor   enemy
       engagement   automobile   instructor

Study Skills, Part Two—Read the study skills passage again, paying special
attention to the lesson being taught. Then, without looking back at the passage,
complete each sentence below by writing in the missing word or words. Check
the Answer Key on page 108 for the answers to Study Skills, Part One, and
Study Skills, Part Two.

1. In a Switch paragraph, the reader looks in the middle of the paragraph to
   find the _____ .

2. In the sample paragraph, the pros and cons of having an automobile
   on _____ are discussed.

3. The paragraph begins with the reasons in favor and ends with the
   reasons _____ .

4. The main idea of the paragraph states that a car can interfere with a student's
   _____ and money.

5. The main idea is used to make a _____ from one side to the other.

15 | Hiroshima— Death and Rebirth, II

by C. E. Maine

Vocabulary—The five words below are from the story you are about to read. Study the words and their meanings. Then complete the ten sentences that follow, using one of the five words to fill in the blank in each sentence. Mark your answer by writing the letter of the word on the line before the sentence. Check your answers in the Answer Key on page 108.

A. animation: spirit; verve

B. environs: surrounding area

C. apprehension: dread

D. despaired: lacked hope

E. copious: abundant

_____ 1. The doctors _____ of saving any victims who were vomiting frequently.

_____ 2. Survivors of the bomb waited with _____ as the American Army of Occupation moved into Hiroshima.

_____ 3. When American doctors arrived in Hiroshima, they found _____ evidence of the harmful effects of radiation.

_____ 4. After a night in the park, many of the wounded showed no signs of _____ .

_____ 5. The _____ of Yoshio's boyhood home were devastated by the bomb.

_____ 6. After searching the rubble near his home, Yoshio _____ of ever seeing his mother or father again.

_____ 7. Surprisingly, many residents of Hiroshima returned to the _____ of their old homes.

_____ 8. Hope that a rescue ship was on its way lent _____ to the survivors in the park.

_____ 9. When Yoshio became sick, doctors were filled with _____ about his future.

_____ 10. Most survivors of the atomic bomb had _____ reasons to despise the United States.

The morality of dropping the bomb has haunted the minds of all thinking people.

Toward evening a small naval launch came up the river. On the deck an officer with a megaphone announced that a naval hospital ship was on its way to rescue survivors. The boost in the morale of the people in the park was tremendous; for the first time Yoshio detected signs of optimism and animation. But no hospital ship ever came.

He slept uneasily that night. His cousin had been vomiting again, as had so many of the other heat-flash victims. In the morning when he awoke he found her dead—just one of hundreds who had died overnight.

Weighed down with fatigue and sorrow, Yoshio left the girl's body in the care of a family who had spent the night near by, and decided to make his way back toward the city center. The fire had now burned itself out. Only twenty-four hours earlier, he reminded himself, Hiroshima had been a busy bustling city starting on a new day, and now it had practically vanished off the face of the earth. At a thousand meters from the epicenter he saw trains that had been hurled like toys many yards from their tracks, trams that had been lifted and dropped onto flattened buildings, and even the bridge by which he entered the city had had its concrete roadway shifted in its entirety.

Near the epicenter what was left of the city was a vast crematorium. Small heaps of ashes indicated where people had been totally consumed where they stood at the moment of the explosion. Perhaps even more macabre were the shadows of people and things etched onto scorched concrete walls by the heat-flash. Thus was immortalized the shadow of a painter, his brush raised, and the shadows of a carter and his horse. Ceramic tiles, with a melting point of 1,300 degrees centigrade, had dissolved. Marble tombstones had been uprooted and flung as though made of cardboard.

Yoshio, in common with his fellow citizens at that time, had no idea what could have caused this incredible holocaust. It was assumed that many bombs must have been dropped simultaneously in one place, and not for many days was it to be rumored that a completely new kind of explosive in a single bomb had been used.

After a thorough search of the environs of his former home and the house of his aunt and uncle, Yoshio gave up the hopeless task. He had to reconcile himself to the fact that he was now alone in the world. The most useful thing he could do under the circumstances would be to go to the Red Cross Hospital and offer to help in any way he could.

No relief came to Hiroshima until late in the day, and even then neither doctors nor medical supplies arrived. Police and working crews came in from nearby towns to collect thousands of corpses for cremation and set up food centers to distribute rice balls to those refugees who had not eaten since the previous morning. At the Red Cross Hospital Yoshio's offer of assistance was gratefully accepted. As he knew the city so well he was assigned to search the ruins of other hospitals for any medical supplies that might have escaped total destruction. As a matter of policy the doctors were only treating the slightly wounded for they had already discovered that those who were seriously injured or constantly vomiting would die inevitably, whatever was done for them. Another curious effect was that even small wounds would not heal for a long time, but would remain swollen and painful, and highly vulnerable to infection. This was due to the destruction of the white blood cells by radiation, but this was not realized immediately.

Yoshio was partly successful in his search for medical supplies, discovering quantities of mercurochrome and an analgesic which were more than welcome. Visiting one ruined hospital he came upon a small detachment of soldiers from the garrison who asked him for water. All were dreadfully mutilated, with faces burned away and eye sockets hollow. He thought they were probably anti-aircraft gunners who had been looking up into the sky at the time of the explosion. He produced a water bottle but had great difficulty in pouring water into their charred, deformed mouths. Full of pity and horror, he promised to send a doctor to them on his return to the hospital— but, of course, the doctor's reply was as expected: "We have no time to spare for those who are already doomed."

By this time the high mortality rate among those who had suffered no apparent injury was creating apprehension among the survivors. Most doctors thought that blood transfusions were not only useless but possibly harmful, since the patient might continue to bleed once the syringe had been withdrawn. In fact, rest and transfusions were the two main effective treatments for radiation sickness, but only a mere handful of doctors and scientists in the whole of Japan knew anything about it.

Three days after the Hiroshima catastrophe, at 11 A.M. on 9 August, 1945, an American Super-Fortress dropped a second atomic bomb on the industrial city of Nagasaki. As in Hiroshima, every building within a mile radius of the epicenter of the explosion was razed to the ground, apart from a few reinforced concrete structures. The dead in Nagasaki numbered 37,501 and the injured (many of whom died later) 51,580. Hiroshima's toll was higher— 78,150 killed and 58,839 injured. Five days after the second A-bomb, Japan surrendered unconditionally.

Around this time Yoshio, still working at the hospital, was horrified to find his thick black hair falling out in chunks if he combed it or ran his fingers through it. His fatigue increased, and when his temperature rose and remained high for three days the doctors ordered him to bed. For two weeks he lay there, during which time his white blood cell count fell to such a low level that the doctors despaired of saving him, but as he had worked so willingly and hard for the hospital he was given the most careful and dedicated treatment available, including liver injections and copious quantities of vitamins.

After the Japanese capitulation the American doctors moved in at high speed to Hiroshima and Nagasaki to gain first-hand medical experience about the effects of the A-bomb, about which little was known. They also brought medical supplies and blood plasma, from which Yoshio benefited and slowly made a recovery.

Meanwhile, many of the people who had been terrified to return to Hiroshima had decided to come back and build again in the ruins. It had been rumored that nothing would ever grow again in Hiroshima and that no one could survive there for at least seven—some believed seventy— years. Nevertheless, there was a steady trickle of returning citizens, though not to the devastated center of the town. Homes were skillfully constructed from the plentiful wreckage, and in a surprisingly short time Hiroshima, despite the lack of electricity, trams, and trains, came back to life. And though the vegetation had been burned, the roots were apparently stimulated by the radiation so that in the season after the bomb weeds grew to rain-forest dimensions all over the city.

A pleasant surprise awaited Yoshio when he was finally well enough to be discharged from the hospital. Instead of going back to his former newspaper delivery round, he was offered a job on the staff of the paper itself, the *Choguku Shimbun,* Hiroshima's own "daily." Astonishingly the newspaper was in production again, though the type was being cast in the open air and an air-raid shelter served as a photographic darkroom. For young Yoshio it was the start of a new life and a new career which suited him well.

Reconstruction work in Hiroshima was hampered by nature itself. On 17 September there was a cloudburst, and twenty-four hours later the electricity power station, which had only been functioning for a few days, broke down. Nearly all the shacks, newly rebuilt and hastily put together, were blown down by hurricanes or washed away by floods.

This latest series of disasters might have been expected to break the spirit of the people, but they rallied and set to work undoing the damage and continuing rebuilding. They were accustomed to flooding, for Hiroshima is built on islands separated by the seven tributaries of the Ohta River, and floods are common enough in the rainy season.

Toward the end of September the American Army of Occupation moved in—an event feared by most of the inhabitants, who no doubt expected brutality and rape. The people of Hiroshima sent away their wives and children, locked their doors, and went nervously to work on the day the "foreign devils" arrived. The Americans, for their part, naturally anticipated more hatred and bitterness in Hiroshima (and Nagasaki) than anywhere else in Japan.

The mechanized columns rolled in at midday, and it was not long before the G.I.s were breaking the ice by handing out chocolate to the children. The citizens themselves, mainly Buddhists, seemed stoically reconciled to the fate which had dealt them such a terrible blow, and they greeted the Americans with courtesy and even hospitality.

From that point on Hiroshima settled down to a more normal life, and today is a thriving modern city with few signs of the scars of a half century ago. The American estimate of deaths at the time (78,150) is likely to be too low a figure as people continued to die from the effects of radiation for a long time afterward. The total death toll is probably nearer to 100,000.

Many of the survivors of the bomb were known as "keloids" from the pink rubbery scars left from the heat-flash burns. Despite the horrors they had suffered, survivors continued to return to Hiroshima, whose population had been reduced to one-third after the bomb. But there were also casualties of a different kind—orphans. Bands of orphan boys turned to the streets to make a good living from black-market deals and even less respectable employment. The guileless Americans were a ready source of supply and demand, and had it not been for them these neglected youngsters would not have found their new way of life so successful. Yoshio himself, with a secure job, felt himself lucky, and spent a great deal of his spare time with these rootless boys, trying to settle them in employment and helping them in other ways.

The spiritual harm to the city of Hiroshima lasted for many years after the dropping of the bomb, the morality of which has exercised the minds of humanists, and indeed all thinking people, since 6 August, 1945. There is perhaps one justification—it has been estimated by military experts that the use of the atomic bomb shortened the war in the Pacific by a year, and saved the lives of a million American troops and a quarter of a million British.

Starting Time		Finishing Time	
Reading Time		Reading Rate	
Comprehension		Vocabulary	

Comprehension— Read the following questions and statements. For each one, put an *x* in the box before the option that contains the most complete or accurate answer. Check your answers in the Answer Key on page 108.

1. A common reaction to the heat flash was
   - ☐ a. blindness.
   - ☐ b. vomiting.
   - ☐ c. loss of appetite.
   - ☐ d. loss of sleep.

2. Despite their desire to help the victims,
   - ☐ a. most of the doctors could not be reached.
   - ☐ b. few doctors knew how to treat radiation.
   - ☐ c. many nurses left the hospital.
   - ☐ d. doctors did not want to take risks.

3. An atomic bomb was dropped on Nagasaki
   - ☐ a. the day after the bombing of Hiroshima.
   - ☐ b. three days after the bombing of Hiroshima.
   - ☐ c. five days after the bombing of Hiroshima.
   - ☐ d. one week after the bombing of Hiroshima.

4. This selection focuses on the
   - ☐ a. aftermath of a terrible event.
   - ☐ b. dedication and altruism of medical professionals.
   - ☐ c. trauma suffered by one person.
   - ☐ d. insensitivity of the United States in dealing with another country.

5. The manner in which Hiroshima and Nagasaki began to return to normalcy was a
   - ☐ a. result of international pressure.
   - ☐ b. consequence of American aid.
   - ☐ c. credit to the Japanese spirit.
   - ☐ d. result of religious tradition.

6. The announcement of the hospital ship could have been
   - ☐ a. an economic blunder.
   - ☐ b. an enemy rumor.
   - ☐ c. a cruel hoax.
   - ☐ d. a psychological ploy.

7. The most serious injuries Yoshio suffered were
   - ☐ a. initially invisible.
   - ☐ b. superficial.
   - ☐ c. quick to heal.
   - ☐ d. around his face and neck.

8. The overall tone of the selection is
   - ☐ a. depressing.
   - ☐ b. frightening.
   - ☐ c. sober.
   - ☐ d. shrill.

9. Convinced that he was the sole survivor of his family, Yoshio
   - ☐ a. vowed personal revenge.
   - ☐ b. retreated within himself.
   - ☐ c. relieved the sufferings of others.
   - ☐ d. became confused with sorrow.

10. The reader is made to relive the events of Hiroshima
   - ☐ a. by means of documented reports.
   - ☐ b. through the eyes of Yoshio.
   - ☐ c. through the Red Cross.
   - ☐ d. through Japanese news reports.

Comprehension Skills

1. recalling specific facts	6. making a judgment
2. retaining concepts	7. making an inference
3. organizing facts	8. recognizing tone
4. understanding the main idea	9. understanding characters
5. drawing a conclusion	10. appreciation of literary forms

Study Skills, Part One—Following is a passage with blanks where words have been omitted. Next to the passage are groups of five words, one group for each blank. Complete the passage by selecting the correct word for each of the blanks.

The Classic Paragraph

This next pattern of paragraph development differs also from those we have been discussing but in a different way. The Classic paragraph presents the ___(1)___ on both ends.

In the Classic paragraph, the main idea statement appears first, followed by the facts, details, etc. Then at the end, the main idea is ___(2)___ or restated.

(1) socialization generalization
     introduction calculation realization

(2) resumed retreated
     repeated reversed reacted

Graphically, the Classic looks like this:

MAIN IDEA
FACTS
DETAILS
EXPLANATION
MAIN IDEA RESTATED

Here is an example of the Classic:

In my opinion, what dampens zeal for reading more than anything else is the fact that youngsters do not spend enough __(3)__ reading. Social activities, movies, and television absorb a disproportionate amount of their time. Nothing succeeds like success, and in this matter of reading the enjoyment from books enhances and spurs on the __(4)__ for further reading experience. But the __(5)__ comes only from mastery, mastery comes only through habit, and habit is formed in only one way; by __(6)__ . One must read and read and read to generate a liking for reading, and a settled habit for reading.

This pattern makes life easy for the reader. It gives him __(7)__ chances at the main idea. Even if he tried, he couldn't miss seeing the author's point.

(3) energy   money
   time   leisure   emotion

(4)   trust   distaste
   detail   desire   reward

(5)   pleasure   defeat
   knowledge   difficulty   cooperation

(6)   alteration   repetition
   competition   explanation   introduction

(7)   no   two
   four   light   three

Study Skills, Part Two—Read the study skills passage again, paying special attention to the lesson being taught. Then, without looking back at the passage, complete each sentence below by writing in the missing word or words. Check the Answer Key on page 108 for the answers to Study Skills, Part One, and Study Skills, Part Two.

1. The Classic paragraph presents the main idea at both _____ .

2. The main idea statement is followed by facts and _____ before it is restated.

3. The example given of the Classic paragraph states that too much time is given to social activities, movies, and _____ .

4. The main idea of the sample paragraph is that more time should be given to _____ .

5. The Classic paragraph gives the reader a second _____ to find the main idea.

16 | The Peter Principle

*by Dr. Lawrence J. Peter
and Raymond Hull*

Vocabulary—The five words below are from the story you are about to read. Study the words and their meanings. Then complete the ten sentences that follow, using one of the five words to fill in the blank in each sentence. Mark your answer by writing the letter of the word on the line before the sentence. Check your answers in the Answer Key on page 108.

A. incompetent: unqualified

B. complied: agreed; acquiesced

C. incoherent: unclear and without order

D. inadvertently: unintentionally

E. contemporary: current

    _____ 1. The principal at the school where the author taught did not want anyone _____ stepping on the rose beds.

    _____ 2. In _____ society, many people hold positions for which they are not well suited.

    _____ 3. People often give _____ answers to questions they do not understand.

    _____ 4. Most people who are promoted have _____ with the rules of their employer.

    _____ 5. Employers routinely promote a person until that person proves to be _____ at his or her job.

    _____ 6. Teaching is not the only profession which contains _____ workers.

    _____ 7. The author received a letter notifying him that he had not _____ with the regulation requiring documents to be registered at the Post Office.

    _____ 8. _____ businesses often promote people for the wrong reasons.

    _____ 9. As superintendent of works, J. S. Minion ended up delivering _____ messages to and from his subordinates.

    _____ 10. E. Tinker _____ alienated both his workers and his customers.

When I was a boy I was taught that the men upstairs knew what they were doing. I was told, "Peter, the more you know, the further you go." So I stayed in school until I graduated from college then went forth into the world clutching firmly these ideas and my new teaching certificate. During the first year of teaching I was upset to find that a number of teachers, school principals, supervisors, and superintendents appeared to be unaware of their professional responsibilities and incompetent in executing their duties. For example, my principal's main concerns were that all window shades be at the same level, that classrooms should be quiet, and that no one step on or near the rose beds. The superintendent's main concerns were that no minority group, no matter how fanatical, should ever be offended and that all official forms be submitted on time. The children's education appeared farthest from the administrator's mind.

At first I thought this was a special weakness of the school system in which I taught, so I applied for certification in another province. I filled out the special forms, enclosed the required documents, and complied willingly with all the red tape. Several weeks later, back came my application and all the documents!

No, there was nothing wrong with my credentials; the forms were correctly filled out; an official departmental stamp showed that they had been received in good order. But an accompanying letter said, "The new regulations require that such forms cannot be accepted by the Department of Education unless they have been registered at the Post Office to ensure safe delivery. Will you please remail the forms to the Department, making sure to register them this time?"

I began to suspect that the local school system did not have a monopoly on incompetence.

As I looked further afield, I saw that every organization contained a number of persons who could not do their jobs.

A Universal Phenomenon

Occupational incompetence is everywhere. Have you noticed it? Probably we all have noticed it.

We see indecisive politicians posing as resolute statesmen and the "authoritative source" who blames his misinformation on "situational imponderables." Limitless are the public servants who are indolent and insolent, military commanders whose behavioral timidity belies their dreadnaught rhetoric, and governors whose innate servility prevents their actually governing. In our sophistication, we virtually shrug aside the immoral cleric, corrupt judge, incoherent attorney, author who cannot write, and English teacher who cannot spell. At universities we see

Occupational incompetence is everywhere. Have you noticed?

proclamations authored by administrators whose own office communications are hopelessly muddled, and droning lectures from inaudible or incomprehensible instructors.

Seeing incompetence at all levels of every hierarchy—political, legal, educational, and industrial—I hypothesized that the cause was some inherent feature of the rules governing the placement of employees. Thus began my serious study of the ways in which employees move upward through a hierarchy, and of what happens to them after promotion.

For my scientific data hundreds of case histories were collected. Here are three typical examples.

J. S. Minion was a maintenance foreman in the public works department of Excelsior City. He was a favorite of the senior officials at City Hall. They all praised his unfailing affability.

"I like Minion," said the superintendent of works. "He has good judgment and is always pleasant and agreeable."

This behavior was appropriate for Minion's position: he was not supposed to make policy, so he had no need to disagree with his superiors.

The superintendent of works retired and Minion succeeded him. Minion continued to agree with everyone. He passed to his foreman every suggestion that came from above. The resulting conflicts in policy, and the continual changing of plans, soon demoralized the department. Complaints poured in from the Mayor and other officials, from taxpayers, and from the maintenance-workers' union.

Minion still says "Yes" to everyone, and carries messages briskly back and forth between his superiors and his subordinates. Nominally a superintendent, he actually does the work of a messenger. The maintenance department regularly exceeds its budget, yet fails to fulfill its program of work. In short, Minion, a competent foreman, became an incompetent superintendent.

E. Tinker was exceptionally zealous and intelligent as an apprentice at G. Reece Auto Repair Inc., and soon rose to journeyman mechanic. In this job he showed outstanding ability in diagnosing obscure faults, and endless patience in correcting them. He was promoted to foreman of the repair shop.

But here his love of things mechanical and his perfectionism become liabilities. He will undertake any job that he thinks looks interesting, no matter how busy the shop may be. "We'll work it in somehow," he says.

He will not let a job go until he is fully satisfied with it.

He meddles constantly. He is seldom to be found at his desk. He is usually up to his elbows in a dismantled motor and while the man who should be doing the work stands watching, other workmen sit around waiting to be assigned new tasks. As a result the shop is always overcrowded with work, always in a muddle, and delivery times are often missed.

Tinker cannot understand that the average customer cares little about perfection—he wants his car back on time! He cannot understand that most of his men are less interested in motors than in their paychecks. So Tinker cannot get on with his customers or with his subordinates. He was a competent mechanic, but is now an incompetent foreman.

Consider the case of the late renowned General A. Goodwin. His hearty, informal manner, his racy style of speech, his scorn for petty regulations, and his undoubted personal bravery made him the idol of his men. He led them to many well-deserved victories.

When Goodwin was promoted to field marshal he had to deal, not with ordinary soldiers, but with politicians and allied generalissimos.

He would not conform to the necessary protocol. He could not turn his tongue to the conventional courtesies and flatteries. He quarreled with all the dignitaries and took to lying for days at a time, drunk and sulking, in his trailer. The conduct of the war slipped out of his hands into those of his subordinates. He had been promoted to a position that he was incompetent to fill.

An Important Clue!

In time I saw that all such cases had a common feature. The employee had been promoted from a position of competence to a position of incompetence. I saw that, sooner or later, this could happen to every employee in every hierarchy.

Suppose you own a pill-rolling factory, Perfect Pill Incorporated. Your foreman pill roller dies of a perforated ulcer. You need a replacement. You naturally look among your rank-and-file pill rollers.

Miss Oval, Mrs. Cylinder, Mr. Ellipse, and Mr. Cube all show various degrees of incompetence. They will naturally be ineligible for promotion. You will choose—other things being equal—your most competent pill roller, Mr. Sphere, and promote him to foreman.

Now suppose Mr. Sphere proves competent as foreman. Later, when your general foreman, Legree, moves up to Works Manager, Sphere will be eligible to take his place.

If, on the other hand, Sphere is an incompetent foreman, he will get no more promotions. He has reached what I call his "level of incompetence." He will stay there till the end of his career.

Some employees, like Ellipse and Cube, reach a level of incompetence in the lowest grade and are never promoted. Some, like Sphere (assuming he is not a satisfactory foreman), reach it after one promotion.

E. Tinker, the automobile repair shop foreman, reached his level of incompetence on the third stage of the hierarchy. General Goodwin reached his level of incompetence at the very top of the hierarchy.

So my analysis of hundreds of cases of occupational incompetence led me on to formulate *The Peter Principle:*
IN A HIERARCHY EVERY EMPLOYEE TENDS TO RISE TO HIS LEVEL OF INCOMPETENCE

A New Science!

Having formulated the Principle, I discovered that I had inadvertently founded a new science, hierarchiology, the study of hierarchies.

The term "hierarchy" was originally used to describe the system of church government by priests graded into ranks. The contemporary meaning includes any organization whose members or employees are arranged in order of rank, grade, or class.

Hierarchiology, although a relatively recent discipline, appears to have great applicability to the fields of public and private administration.

This Means You!

My Principle is the key to an understanding of all hierarchal systems, and therefore to an understanding of the whole structure of civilization. A few eccentrics try to avoid getting involved with hierarchies, but everyone in business, industry, trade-unionism, politics, government, the armed forces, religion, and education is so involved. All of them are controlled by the Peter Principle.

Many of them, to be sure, may win a promotion or two, moving from one level of competence to a higher level of competence. But competence in that new position qualifies them for still another promotion. For each individual, for *you,* for *me,* the final promotion is from a level of competence to a level of incompetence.

So, given enough time—and assuming the existence of enough ranks in the hierarchy—each employee rises to, and remains at, his level of incompetence. Peter's Corollary states:

In time, every post tends to be occupied by an employee who is incompetent to carry out its duties.

Who Turns the Wheels?

You will rarely find, of course, a system in which *every* employee has reached his level of incompetence. In most instances, something is being done to further the ostensible purposes for which the hierarchy exists.

Work is accomplished by those employees who have not yet reached their level of incompetence.

Starting Time		Finishing Time	
Reading Time		Reading Rate	
Comprehension		Vocabulary	

Comprehension— Read the following questions and statements. For each one, put an *x* in the box before the option that contains the most complete or accurate answer. Check your answers in the Answer Key on page 108.

1. As a first-year teacher, the author observed that administrators at his school cared little about
   - ☐ a. public opinion.
   - ☐ b. superficial appearances.
   - ☐ c. the quality of students' education.
   - ☐ d. rules and regulations.

2. The author was conditioned to believe that
   - ☐ a. education was for the elite.
   - ☐ b. teachers lacked professionalism.
   - ☐ c. manual labor should be avoided.
   - ☐ d. authority should not be questioned.

3. The author found the science of hierarchiology
   - ☐ a. while struggling through his first year as a teacher.
   - ☐ b. after working as an automobile repair shop foreman.
   - ☐ c. during a chance encounter with J. S. Minion.
   - ☐ d. after noting widespread incompetence in many organizations.

4. The case histories of Minion, Tinker, and Goodwin suggest that
   - ☐ a. competence should determine promotion.
   - ☐ b. people should not be promoted.
   - ☐ c. promotion should not be determined by seniority.
   - ☐ d. journeymen mechanics make incompetent foremen.

5. School administrators seemed unable to distinguish between
   - ☐ a. the important and the unimportant.
   - ☐ b. the minorities and the majority.
   - ☐ c. work and leisure.
   - ☐ d. professionals and nonprofessionals.

6. A person's level of incompetence should be
   - ☐ a. concealed carefully.
   - ☐ b. faced squarely.
   - ☐ c. charitably overlooked.
   - ☐ d. generally tolerated.

7. The author's first year of teaching left him
   - ☐ a. discouraged.
   - ☐ c. indifferent.
   - ☐ b. bitter.
   - ☐ d. disillusioned.

8. The author's presentation is
   - ☐ a. well documented.
   - ☐ b. prejudiced.
   - ☐ c. amusing but pointed.
   - ☐ d. contradictory and embarrassing.

9. A. Goodwin was most happy when
   - ☐ a. drunk.
   - ☐ b. acting as field marshal.
   - ☐ c. holding the rank of general.
   - ☐ d. dealing with politicians.

10. The selection is written in the form of
    - ☐ a. a document.
    - ☐ c. an application.
    - ☐ b. a critique.
    - ☐ d. a eulogy.

Comprehension Skills	
1. recalling specific facts	6. making a judgment
2. retaining concepts	7. making an inference
3. organizing facts	8. recognizing tone
4. understanding the main idea	9. understanding characters
5. drawing a conclusion	10. appreciation of literary forms

Study Skills, Part One—Following is a passage with blanks where words have been omitted. Next to the passage are groups of five words, one group for each blank. Complete the passage by selecting the correct word for each of the blanks.

The Thinker Paragraph

This pattern of paragraph development is truly different from any other because the main idea or generalization does not ___(1)___ anywhere—it is not stated.

The Thinker paragraph seeks to create an impression in the reader's mind. The main idea is ___(2)___ rather than stated.

(1)   progress   continue
    appear   stop   lead

(2)   noted   implied
    expressed   questioned   created

Graphically the Thinker looks like this:

```
┌─────────────────────────────┐
│                             │
│           FACTS             │
│                             │
│            OR               │
│                             │
│          DETAILS            │
│                             │
│     (MAIN IDEA IMPLIED)     │
│                             │
└─────────────────────────────┘
```

Here is an example of the Thinker:

Then there are those persons who are temperamentally given to hesitancy of mind, to exaggerating __(3)__ , and to discounting everything that bears the semblance of truth. These temperamental skeptics come to prize their doubting as a sign of a nicely adjusted mentality. Indeed, after a while they regard any definite, __(4)__ statement as an evidence of coarseness of mind, as some departure from the neutrality of the wise spectator. They assume the aloofness of a detached __(5)__ ; judging, examining, approving, condemning, but never yielding to the temptation of a determined __(6)__ .

In this example, there is no one statement inclusive or general enough to represent the thought of the entire paragraph. All of the sentences taken __(7)__ contribute to the idea communicated.

| (3) | difficulties | opportunities |
| | friendships | occasions | relations |

| (4) | interesting | related |
| | negative | encouraging | positive |

| (5) | participant | follower |
| | enemy | observer | believer |

| (6) | question | defeat |
| | demand | chance | choice |

| (7) | apart | together |
| | separately | gradually | rapidly |

Study Skills, Part Two—Read the study skills passage again, paying special attention to the lesson being taught. Then, without looking back at the passage, complete each sentence below by writing in the missing word or words. Check the Answer Key on page 108 for the answers to Study Skills, Part One, and Study Skills, Part Two.

1. The main idea of the Thinker paragraph is not _____ .

2. The author tries to create an _____ in the reader's mind.

3. In the sample paragraph, the author discusses those people who

   consider _____ to be a sign of well-adjusted mentality.

4. They prefer to employ the _____ of the wise spectators.

5. In this kind of paragraph, no one statement is inclusive enough or

   _____ enough to represent the main idea.

17 | The Return of the Salmon

by Betty W. Carter

Vocabulary—The five words below are from the story you are about to read. Study the words and their meanings. Then complete the ten sentences that follow, using one of the five words to fill in the blank in each sentence. Mark your answer by writing the letter of the word on the line before the sentence. Check your answers in the Answer Key on page 108.

A. progeny: offspring

B. elude: evade

C. wantonly: unrestrainedly

D. comprehended: understood

E. comprised: included; contained

_____ 1. A salmon's _____ will return to their birthplace to mate and spawn.

_____ 2. People no longer _____ pollute the water of the Fraser River.

_____ 3. After careful study, people finally _____ why the salmon population dropped dramatically in the 1910s.

_____ 4. Newly hatched salmon _____ predators by traveling under the cover of darkness.

_____ 5. The salmon of the Pacific Ocean are _____ of many different races.

_____ 6. If all goes well, a salmon's _____ will live four years.

_____ 7. Only those salmon which _____ fishing nets live long enough to produce offspring.

_____ 8. No construction workers in 1913 _____ the danger their work posed to salmon.

_____ 9. Zooplankton chiefly _____ a young salmon's diet.

_____ 10. With the creation of strict international limits, fishermen could no longer fish _____ for sockeye salmon.

There's a gold rush going on in the glacier-fed rivers of Canada's British Columbia, high above Vancouver.

The Caribou Trail slogged by prospectors 110 years ago is useless now, and the easily found gold metal in the Fraser River has long since panned out. But the cold, rushing brooks of the Fraser watershed still hold

GEORGE ROBBINS

With nations working together, the golden fish of the North are prospering.

a great natural resource: the gold-red salmon which pair and spawn on the river's gravel beds. And now that man has learned to understand the salmon's life cycle, it's a gold rush that need never end.

Not that the spawners mean immediate wealth: the law today protects them in the spawning channels and in any river they use. But the adult sockeye salmon, harvested by both U.S. and Canadian seiners, trollers, and netters in the salt waters of the Juan de Fuca Strait (along which runs the boundary between Canada and the United States), is a welcome delicacy of both countries.

Oil refineries in the Fraser watershed area, using special water recycling techniques, make sure that the salmon's vital spawning waters are not polluted. Other local industries take equal care with the fragile birthplace environment of the sockeye salmon. Strict salmon catch regulations insure that future generations of salmon will not be decimated.

A Mysterious Life Cycle

The Fraser watershed is one of the greatest salmon nurseries in the world. Clear brooklets rush west and east respectively over beds of rounded pebbles, part of the debris left behind when the Ice Age ended. These gravel-bedded streams are spawning grounds for the Fraser's Pacific salmon—Fraser because they're spawned in the Fraser's tributaries, Pacific because they spend three of their usual four years of life in the Pacific Ocean.

Returning from the Pacific to the stream where they were born, the salmon travel upstream as much as 17 miles a day. Intuitively, the sockeye swim past many tributary entrances, to turn at last into that one little river where their own life began and where, having given life, they soon die.

With her tail, the female flails out a depression, called a redd, into which her eggs will fall. Two by two the paired sockeye lie quiet, brilliant in their spawning colors of red and bright green. With a tremor, the female deposits her eggs and the male moves closer to release the fertilizing milt which clouds over the redd. The female then moves upstream to slap out a new depression; the bubbling water carries fine pebbles and sand downstream where they cover the eggs, pink and fertile. (A few other eggs, improperly covered and sun-bleached, float with the current, food for the waiting herring gulls that come 300 miles inland for the feast.)

Within two days, the salmon consummate the reason for their pilgrimage from the sea and lose their vivid spawning colors. The male drifts away; the female steadies her body above the redd for as long as she has the strength. Then, exhausted, she too drifts downstream. Eighteen days after entering the spawning stream, the salmon die. Their bodies fertilize the zooplankton on which the salmon's own progeny will feed.

Safe under the gravel, salmon hatch from the eggs in February. Fed from the yolk sac to which they are attached, their only external need is a flow of pure oxygen-bearing water. Finally, on a moonless night in the spring, inch-long fry will wriggle up through the egg-holding gravel.

Under cover of darkness, they elude predator fish and make their way to a nearby rearing lake—which is as important to sockeye production as the clear, cold spawning beds. A year later, the young salmon are ready for their voyage to the sea.

In the estuary, the sockeye adjust to salt water: for three years they will graze in the pastures of the Pacific Ocean, roaming perhaps 2,000 miles from the small river where they were spawned.

Four years later, guided by as yet unidentified navigational aids, the sleek sockeye salmon will return to the Fraser River through the Juan de Fuca Strait.

From the time they reenter fresh water until their death, the sockeye eat nothing; their bodies are fortified with stored fat before they begin their long struggle to their upstream spawning grounds. Because they are farther from the sea than most varieties of salmon, the red flesh of the sockeye is richer than that of most salmon and has long been a prized delicacy. The fish are at their prime as they pass through the fishing fleet.

Dangerous Years for the Salmon

The Fraser has always been a salmon river, rich in pink, chinook or spring, coho, and chum salmon as well as the dominant sockeye. But in 1913, a man-made disaster struck.

A railway bed was being blasted from the steep sides of the scenic canyon high above the Fraser. Wantonly, thoughtlessly, the workmen shoved the debris from the bed into the river.

Millions of sockeye which had escaped the fishing boats were on their way to the Adams and other rivers to spawn. Now, blocked by rocks and current, the sockeye milled helplessly below the stricture. Their spawning time came—and passed. They couldn't pair because they could not reach their ancient spawning grounds. They died—

and with them their progeny which would have returned four years later, and those which would have returned faithfully every four years thereafter.

In 1914, the year following the disaster, another slide blocked the secondary Adams River run.

Each race of sockeye has its dominant year, its secondary, and two years in which the number of spawners reaching the grounds is negligible. The elimination of both the secondary and the dominant runs meant that the Adams River race, one of the most productive, nearly became extinct.

But the long-term consequences of the disasters were not immediately comprehended. While the catches in succeeding cycle years were alarmingly small, the cause of the slump was said by some to be that the fishermen had overfished.

The catch of Fraser River sockeye fell sharply: from an average per-year catch of 9½ million from 1898 to 1913, it fell to 1.2 million between 1921 and 1924. It seemed that a great natural resource was about to be lost, played out by man's carelessness.

How the Fraser salmon had been brought back, and how the Fraser River has become a multiuse river, constitutes a vivid story of man's efforts to live successfully within, and cooperate with, a delicate ecological balance. In the Fraser river story there is an added factor of cooperation successfully achieved between two great nations, Canada and the United States.

The Salmon Come Back

In 1930 Canada and the United States signed a historic convention for the protection, preservation, and extension of the sockeye salmon fisheries of the Fraser River system. Under its terms the trailblazing International Pacific Salmon Fisheries Commission was appointed, comprised equally of U.S. citizens and Canadians.

By the terms of the compact, the International Pacific Salmon Fisheries Commission was not permitted to take action or regulate the catch until it had devoted eight years to research. Well before that time was up, the Commission had pinpointed the railroad bed catastrophe as a major factor in the salmon's decline.

As its first act, the Commission installed specially designed fishways to help overcome the congestion caused by the slides. These are concrete sluices with rectangular slots opening at the down-river end. At a given stage of the river, the fish automatically enter the only set of slots available at that depth. Once inside the sluice, the salmon swim along the fishway until the passage opens into the river beyond the obstruction it was designed to circumvent.

Subsequently, the Commission began regulating the catch of sockeye salmon, *race by race*. Each race returns to its own particular river, which gives the race its name and identity. Each race is so definitely unique that the markings on its scales are different from those on any other race's—as sure as identification of the race as the sworls on a man's fingerprints.

Regulations of the catch and erection of fishways are holding operations for protection of existent sockeye. To increase production of adult fish, artificial spawning channels have been devised and are proving amazingly efficient. In these artificial channels, the return of adult salmon has been almost six times greater than for eggs spawned in natural beds.

Refineries: Good Neighbors for the Salmon

In any watershed today, the Pacific salmon face three potential dangers they did not face a century ago: irrigation requirements, hydroelectric dams, and man-made pollution. It seems that almost every step man takes involves possible environmental pollution. Each of these steps must therefore be taken very carefully.

A log drive during a low water stage can tear up gravel beds, leave bark caught in the pebbles, and start erosion in curving banks—which will flush silt onto the fragile salmon eggs. A pulp mill's improperly treated effluent could mean death to an approaching run of salmon. A town's sewage disposal could eliminate oxygen in a river. Farmers' pesticides, washed from productive fields, could make a river unproductive.

When a new industrial plant is to be erected, the Commission works with management to see that plans and specifications are carefully tailored to insure the protection of the Fraser River salmon. Later, the Commission checks periodically to make sure that effluent-control devices are performing their job of salmon-protection efficiently. Human cooperation keeps the salmon safe.

For example, when the first oil refinery in the watershed was built, at Brocklehurst near Kamloops where the Thompson and Fraser Rivers join, the state of technology of effluent disposal was just emerging. The best known way to dispose of refinery waste water was through evaporation lagoons. This proved a practical method for this small plant; there was sufficient ground available, and the geology of the site permitted it. Half a mile from the salmon river, the oil refinery can operate without fear of contaminating the vital water.

When the second oil refinery was built at St. George, where the Nechako and the Fraser Rivers meet, it was designed so that waste water reaches the Fraser only after extensive treatment. This guarantees that the water will be harmless to the fish. Water that has been in contact with oil is stripped of volatile hydrocarbons, solids, and hydrogen sulfide. Then, the total refinery effluent goes through a gravity settler before it is oxidized. From the biological oxidation pond, the water passes into seepage pits, from which it percolates through layers of sandy soil and thence safely into the river.

Today, the salmon swim safely past the great industrial complexes, and spawn securely in streams used also for logging and as water for increasing numbers of pulp mills. The hard lesson of 1913 has been well learned. Care, research, and planning have replaced the blind, surging pattern of growth of both nations' earlier days.

When care replaces thoughtlessness, man may have the best of two worlds: the energy and products of industry that he desires, and the clean, verdant world which is his heritage. The spawning Fraser River salmon is a living reminder of this happy ecological truth.

Starting Time		Finishing Time	
Reading Time		Reading Rate	
Comprehension		Vocabulary	

Comprehension— Read the following questions and statements. For each one, put an *x* in the box before the option that contains the most complete or accurate answer. Check your answers in the Answer Key on page 108.

1. Fraser's Pacific salmon return to their birthplace via
   □ a. the Caribou Trail.   □ c. Nechako river.
   □ b. Juan de Fuca strait.   □ d. Thompson river.

2. Fraser's Pacific salmon have
   □ a. an unusually long life.
   □ b. a strong, gamey taste.
   □ c. an amazing sense of direction.
   □ d. a bleak, uncertain future.

3. The sockeye salmon hatched in the Fraser River return to their spawning ground
   □ a. once.   □ c. three times.
   □ b. twice.   □ d. four times.

4. The survival of the sockeye salmon depends on
   □ a. man's commitment to conservation.
   □ b. United States and Canadian fishermen.
   □ c. banishing industries from the watershed.
   □ d. the vagaries of tide and current.

5. Before the establishment of the International Pacific Salmon Fisheries Commission, sockeye salmon were
   □ a. getting caught in concrete sluices.
   □ b. overrunning the Fraser watershed area.
   □ c. in danger of extinction.
   □ d. suffering from an undiagnosed disease.

6. The stages in the life cycle of the salmon reveal
   □ a. their unpredictable nature.
   □ b. the futility of life.
   □ c. the cruelty of nature.
   □ d. a balance of nature.

7. Industry and oil refineries
   □ a. damage the environment irreparably.
   □ b. contribute to the purity of the air we breathe.
   □ c. do not work for their best interests.
   □ d. need not be at odds with nature.

8. The selection ends on a note of
   □ a. self-satisfaction.   □ c. apology.
   □ b. disappointment.   □ d. cautious optimism.

9. The workers who dumped debris into the Fraser River were
   □ a. ignorant of the needs of salmon.
   □ b. cruel and malicious.
   □ c. victims of their employers.
   □ d. plagued by guilty consciences.

10. Which of the following phrases from the selection contains an alliteration?
   □ a. "sleek sockeye salmon will return to the Fraser River"
   □ b. "the bubbling water carries fine pebbles and sand downstream"
   □ c. "the Commission had pinpointed the railroad bed catastrophe"
   □ d. "oil is stripped of volatile hydrocarbons, solids, and hydrogen sulfide"

Comprehension Skills
1. recalling specific facts   6. making a judgment
2. retaining concepts   7. making an inference
3. organizing facts   8. recognizing tone
4. understanding the main idea   9. understanding characters
5. drawing a conclusion   10. appreciation of literary forms

Study Skills, Part One—Following is a passage with blanks where words have been omitted. Next to the passage are groups of five words, one group for each blank. Complete the passage by selecting the correct word for each of the blanks.

Understanding Dictionaries, I

It is generally taken for granted that everyone knows how to use a dictionary. In reality, though, very few students can use one well or effectively.

While it is true that students can locate the entry (word) they are looking for, it is also true that most of them cannot translate the information they find into ___(1)___ form. The result is that many students will take the ___(2)___ meaning given whether or not it makes sense in a particular context.

Take a few moments to become familiar with your dictionary. For each word entry, the ___(3)___ of items given may vary slightly from one dictionary to the next, but the following information can usually be found.

1. Entry Word. The word you are looking up is shown in bold type, ___(4)___ than the rest of the copy in the entry. In many dictionaries, the word overhangs or sticks out a little into the left margin to help you find it easily.

Words that are spelled alike but are unrelated are listed ___(5)___ . The word *bow*, for example, would be listed as three entries: (1) a *bow* to the audience, (2) a *bow* and arrow, and (3) the *bow* (front end) of a ship.

In addition to general words of the English language, most dictionaries include commonly used ___(6)___ words and expressions; the names of historical characters, artists, writers, and other famous people; and many geographic locations. In special sections of your dictionary you can often find lists of colleges and universities; tables of weights and ___(7)___ , lists of signs, symbols, and abbreviations; and articles on grammar, usage, and spelling. In this respect, a dictionary is like a small, concise encyclopedia.

(1)	usable		acceptable
	exceptional	ultimate	understandable

(2)	familiar		favorite
	last	easiest	first

(3)	choice		number
	order	quality	kind

(4)	longer		higher
	stronger	larger	smaller

(5)	together		continuously
	separately	partially	sequentially

(6)	local		foreign
	national	familiar	educational

(7)	places		times
	buildings	measures	words

Study Skills, Part Two—Read the study skills passage again, paying special attention to the lesson being taught. Then, without looking back at the passage, complete each sentence below by writing in the missing word or words. Check the Answer Key on page 108 for the answers to Study Skills, Part One, and Study Skills, Part Two.

1. Very few students can use a dictionary well or _____ .

2. Most students take the first meaning given whether it makes _____ in a particular context or not.

3. The entry word is usually printed in different type from the rest of the copy so that it can be easily _____ .

4. Words that are spelled alike but are _____ are not listed together.

5. Special sections containing information make some dictionaries similar to _____ .

The Fight to Stop Torture

by James David Barber

Vocabulary—The five words below are from the story you are about to read. Study the words and their meanings. Then complete the ten sentences that follow, using one of the five words to fill in the blank in each sentence. Mark your answer by writing the letter of the word on the line before the sentence. Check your answers in the Answer Key on page 108.

A. verified: confirmed

B. bolster: boost; support

C. tactics: techniques

D. starkly: grimly; bluntly

E. leverage: power to act effectively

_____ 1. Torture is one of the _____ some governments use to maintain control of their people.

_____ 2. The United States should use its _____ to demand an end to torture around the world.

_____ 3. Amnesty International has _____ cases of torture in many different countries.

_____ 4. Public relations firms try to _____ the public image of their customers.

_____ 5. The truth about the Turkish government stands out _____ against the international image it cultivates.

_____ 6. Public condemnation is one of the most effective _____ in the fight against torture.

_____ 7. A private citizen like Laura Bonaparte often has little _____ when it comes to dealing with the police.

_____ 8. South Korea has been anxious to _____ its reputation among Americans.

_____ 9. Victims of torture are forced to face their torturers _____ , without the benefit of lawyers, doctors, or family members.

_____ 10. Some reports of torture are not easily _____ .

America is a caring country. When drought hits the Southeast, farmers in the Midwest send hay—free of charge. Every year, Americans by the millions dig into their own pockets to help the helpless, at home and abroad. We could do more, but through our churches and charities, we do try to demonstrate that we mean what we say when we speak of love and respect for our fellow human beings.

Every day governments around the world are torturing and killing innocent people. Who supports these torturers? As Americans, we don't have to look very far.

No wonder then that it shocks Americans to learn that money we pay for taxes goes into the pockets of dictators who torture their own citizens.

Unbelievable as it sounds, there is no doubt of the truth that American money winds up supporting torturers.

Extensive, detailed, carefully checked reports, spelling out names, dates, and places, are issued by Amnesty International, the worldwide human rights organization. These reports confirm the facts of torture and killing by a wide variety of governments, with different ideologies from left to right. In too many cases, massive U.S. support goes to governments whose current human rights offenses are verified.

Take Turkey, for example. In 1986 alone, our taxes provided $738,841,000 to the Turkish government. Officials there keep claiming they are making "progress" in human rights. In fact, however, hundreds of Turkish citizens are in jail only for what they believe in or what ethnic group they belong to, and many are, at this moment, being subjected to crippling humiliation and pain. Men, women, and children in Turkish prisons are being shocked with electric rods, burnt with cigarettes, and sexually abused—not just now and then, but systematically, hour after hour.

In spite of Amnesty International's repeated appeals, the Turkish authorities still have to put a stop to torture in their jails. Day by day, Amnesty International is receiving new reports of Turkish torture.

Instead of wiping out torture in their police stations, Turkey has hired (at $1,000,000 a year) a high-powered public relations firm in Washington, D.C., Gray and Company, to bolster Turkey's public image and make sure Congress keeps the foreign aid money coming. That company represented "Baby Doc" Duvalier, Haiti's brutal dictator, before his overthrow. Experts in polling, advertising, and lobbying Congress and the Adminis- tration, Gray and Company says it is "proud to count among our professional staff" dozens of former top officials of the U.S. government who know how to influ- ence national policy.

Turkey's tactics are not unique. Another big-time Washington lobby, headed by a former White House aide, was hired by South Korea (at $1,200,000) to "protect, manage, and expand trade and economic interests." Multi-page advertising sections, touting South Korea's economy, appear in news magazines. Meanwhile, South Korea demonstrates its contempt for free speech by locking up dissenters by the hundreds. One of their typical torture methods is to hang people upside down and force water through their nostrils.

The list is long. China, South Africa, Mexico, Morocco, and both the government and the *contras* of Nicaragua have their lobbyists at work in Washington. Such clients spend an estimated $500,000,000 a year to persuade the American people and their elected representatives that they are worthy of American support, in spite of their violations of American values. They outspend human rights organizations like Amnesty International by at least 10 to one.

Why does it matter that these offending governments can recruit professional public relations experts in the U.S.? It matters because, as a recent report by the American Association for the Advancement of Science put it, "The most powerful weapon for preventing the use of torture is the mobilization of international opinion and pressure. It is the 'shame of exposure' that governments fear most." When it is revealed that Castro's Cuba, which advertises itself as a modern civilized nation, imprisoned and tormented prisoners of conscience for decades, the Cuban government gets upset. When Soviet Premier Gorbachev arrives in Paris for high-level talks with France's President Mitterand and is met by demonstrators protesting the U.S.S.R.'s practices of starving, freezing, and drugging prisoners of conscience, he feels he must make an explanation. When world attention focuses on Indonesia because the Reagans are visiting there, and journalists discover that the Suharto government has systematically massacred thousands of people, Indonesia's reputation suffers in every capital around the world. The battle for world opinion is the key to the battle to stop human rights offenses. The public relations experts ought to join that battle on the side of those who demand that torture stop.

Instead, we confront sophisticated and subtle professionals whose strategies well may undercut the human rights movement. Their strongest tactic is diversion. For example, Turkey's lobbyist would rather have you think about their upcoming art exhibit or Turkey's tourist attractions than about their barbaric and degrading abuse of the helpless. When diversion doesn't work, the torturers may simply deny that they abuse prisoners (as Iraq does), despite the evidence, or point to statements in their constitution against torture (as Turkey does), as if their words could make up for their behavior.

When the news of regular, systematic human rights violations comes out, the torturers and their Washington lobbyists dream up theories to justify torture. For instance, they will argue that human rights conditions in their country are getting better—so be patient; or that, once they get their economy in order or their political system straightened out, they will surely stop butchering people. Such arguments will sound familiar to Americans who took part in the civil rights movement and so often were told to slow down and wait.

Other sophisticates will take off from the idea that different cultures naturally behave differently, and so we should not be indignant when some foreign nation has torture as one of its customs. Still others, obsessed with the question of who is most to blame, will be satisfied with delicate comparisons among human rights violators, as if, once we know whom to blame, we will have solved the problem.

Then there are the so-called "realists" who justify cruelty as necessary to protect a nation's security, not just from immediate threats, but from long-term enemies. Such "realists" forget what already has happened to rulers who systematically abused their own people—Hitler, Stalin, Duvalier, Marcos, the Shah of Iran, Somoza, Batista, the Argentine *junta*. In fact, torture undermines security.

These images and arguments in favor of torture can not stand up against a simple truth—as you read this, a person like you is being tortured! A person like you would include Laura Bonaparte's daughter. On Christmas Eve, Laura's phone rang. The voice said her daughter, Noni, had been taken away in an army jeep. Laura contacted the police. They said Noni had been killed in a skirmish with terrorists. Laura demanded her daughter's body. The police brought her a jar with a hand in it.

A person like you would be the father of a 12-year-old boy picked up by the police. The boy was brought home dead, his body marked all over with signs of torture.

A person like you would be a student forced to watch as his aged mother, 73 years old, was stripped naked and beaten, shocked, and burned, screaming in pain, in front of him.

Those are real cases, not made-up stories. All one has to do is to imagine that they describe your daughter, your son, your mother. Then, the fancy arguments justifying torture collapse.

The essential principle of human rights is the integrity of the individual. A person may be described with all sorts of labels, analyzed and categorized in every sort of way, but a person is the opposite of a thing. A person is to be seen as a complete being, a being who, by the right of his or her existence, is to be accorded dignity and respect.

This principle of individual integrity is illustrated starkly in a report from El Salvador in 1980. Six young labor leaders told of their friend who was taken by soldiers,

tortured for days, and killed. His body was torn to pieces and the parts scattered in a ditch. His friends managed to collar the soldiers, "and we took them to the ditch and made them assemble our friend on the ground like a man, and ask forgiveness of the corpse." Then, they quietly let the soldiers go.

By contrast, the torturer's aim is to destroy the integrity of his victim, to transform a person into a thing, to shred his or her dignity. That is what none of us can decently tolerate.

There are no exceptions. The law is clear: "No one shall be subjected to torture or cruel, inhuman, or degrading treatment or punishment," says the International Covenant on Civil and Political Rights. There is no way the rest of us can escape what Albert Camus called "the common lot of pain," unless we are willing to resign from the human race.

The common lot of pain links us to suffering, but it also links us to hope. In the midst of despair and degradation, tortured prisoners again and again have been lifted out of living death by the realization that fellow human beings—even those unknown and far away—are working to rescue them.

In the U.S. alone, Amnesty International has more than 1,500 groups and 300,000 members working to stop torture. Individual appeals for prisoners "adopted" by AI groups have contributed to the release of thousands of prisoners and thousands of others have been saved from torture. Worldwide, Amnesty International demands that every government:
- Order torture stopped under all circumstances.
- Bring every prisoner promptly before a judge and let his or her family, doctor, and lawyer visit him.
- Close down secret prisons and put out accurate information about which prisoners are where.
- Monitor prison procedures. Tell prisoners of their rights and how to register complaints. Inspect the prisons regularly.
- Investigate and report publicly on torture complaints and do not threaten witnesses.
- Throw out of court any statement made under torture.
- Make torturing a criminal offense in all cases.
- Arrest and prosecute alleged torturers wherever they are.
- Train police and military to refuse to torture, even if ordered to do so.
- Help torture victims get medical care, rehabilitation, and financial compensation.
- Press other governments to stop torture. Under no circumstances provide training or other aid for torturers.
- Sign and support international agreements to stop torture.

These specifics make a difference. In October, 1984, Congress passed and the President signed into law a definite American commitment against torture. The law sets out specific requirements for diplomats—to report regularly on human rights abuses overseas and to take specific steps to end them.

Clearly, human rights is now a worldwide concern, part

of nearly every serious international negotiation. That is happening because concerned citizens on every continent have made up their minds not to let national boundaries get in the way of the implementation of our bedrock human values. It is happening because hundreds of thousands of people are not content to stand by and watch while victims are battered into madness and death. It is happening because the human rights movement has gone public, no longer confining itself to behind-the-scenes negotiations.

In the U.S., nearly all of us are descended from people who came here for freedom from the repression of human rights. Today, more and more citizens are raising the key questions with the representatives we send to Washington—our senators and Congressmen: "When is the government going to use its leverage to advance our national commitment to human decency? When are we going to show the world that we mean what we say— that 'all men are created equal' and that human beings everywhere have rights no government has the right to take away from them, namely 'life, liberty, and the pursuit of happiness' "?

Starting Time		Finishing Time	
Reading Time		Reading Rate	
Comprehension		Vocabulary	

Comprehension
— Read the following questions and statements. For each one, put an *x* in the box before the option that contains the most complete or accurate answer. Check your answers in the Answer Key on page 108.

1. The public relations firm Gray and Company
   □ a. has publicly condemned all forms of torture.
   □ b. refused to take on Nicaragua as a client.
   □ c. tries to justify Turkey's actions.
   □ d. is unaware of their clients' position on the issue of torture.

2. Countries such as Turkey are anxious to
   □ a. improve their record of human rights.
   □ b. publicize their human rights record.
   □ c. keep American aid flowing to them.
   □ d. help Amnesty International.

3. Which of the following is *not* a demand made by Amnesty International of governments around the world?
   □ a. the signing of international agreements to stop torture
   □ b. the execution of known torturers
   □ c. the closing of secret prisons
   □ d. the regular inspections of prisons

4. Abuse of citizens is
   □ a. a rare and horrifying event.
   □ b. all too common in many countries.
   □ c. not tolerated by any legitimate government.
   □ d. a regrettable but inevitable part of modern life.

5. Withholding monetary aid from governments which abuse citizens would
   □ a. have a disastrous effect on Third World nations.
   □ b. be an effective way to reduce incidents of torture.
   □ c. do more harm than good.
   □ d. pacify Amnesty International.

6. Governments which torture their citizens should be
   □ a. ignored.   □ c. ridiculed.
   □ b. condemned.   □ d. overthrown.

7. The United States government does not
   □ a. care about human rights.
   □ b. approve of Amnesty International's approach.
   □ c. torture its citizens.
   □ d. support countries which torture its citizens.

8. The author appeals to the reader's sense of
   □ a. guilt.   □ c. honesty.
   □ b. justice.   □ d. pride.

9. Members of Amnesty International are
   □ a. principled.   □ c. patient.
   □ b. timid.   □ d. bitter.

10. The sentence, "Day by day, Amnesty International is receiving new reports of Turkish torture" is an example of
   □ a. overstatement.
   □ b. personification.
   □ c. literal language.
   □ d. allusion.

Comprehension Skills

1. recalling specific facts	6. making a judgment
2. retaining concepts	7. making an inference
3. organizing facts	8. recognizing tone
4. understanding the main idea	9. understanding characters
5. drawing a conclusion	10. appreciation of literary forms

Study Skills, Part One—Following is a passage with blanks where words have been omitted. Next to the passage are groups of five words, one group for each blank. Complete the passage by selecting the correct word for each of the blanks.

Understanding Dictionaries, II

2. Syllabification. How a word is divided into syllables is shown in the entry word. This shows you how to __(1)__ that word (if it is necessary to break it at the end of a line, for example) without looking further.

Dots are used to separate the syllables, and the word can be split at the end of a line only where dots are used. If a word does not show a dot, it cannot be __(2)__ , even though it may be pronounced as two syllables. *Rhythm* is such a word.

Dots are used instead of hyphens to indicate syllables because hyphens are __(3)__ for listing hyphenated words, such as *half-moon*. Naturally, hyphenated words can be divided at the hyphens.

3. Pronunciation. Immediately after the entry word, the pronunciation is shown in parentheses. When two pronunciations are used, the first one is the most __(4)__ .

Symbols and special marks are used to show the correct pronunciation of words. Many of the marks are explained at the bottom of the page in a pronunciation key that uses sample, illustrative words. So don't be __(5)__ when you see unusual spellings and symbols; just refer to the notes at the bottom of the page and you will find a word you know to make the pronunciation __(6)__ to you.

Along with the pronunciation in parentheses, the syllables that should be stressed will be __(7)__ . In multi-syllable words, the syllable having the greatest stress will be designated with a primary mark (′). A secondary stress mark (′) indicates a syllable receiving less stress; and a syllable having relatively weak stress will be unmarked.

(1)	translate		spell
	pronounce	hyphenate	use

(2)		divided		used
	emphasized		added	pronounced

(3)	unnecessary		forbidden
	considered	overlooked	needed

(4)		extraordinary		foreign
	liked		common	attractive

(5)		satisfied		happy
	confused	complaisant		nervous

(6)		difficult		new
	clear	interesting		vague

(7)		omitted		indicated
	generated	implied		needed

Study Skills, Part Two—Read the study skills passage again, paying special attention to the lesson being taught. Then, without looking back at the passage, complete each sentence below by writing in the missing word or words. Check the Answer Key on page 108 for the answers to Study Skills, Part One, and Study Skills, Part Two.

1. In order to hyphenate a word, refer to how the word is divided into

   _____ .

2. A word can be separated at the end of a line only _____ syllables.

3. Pronunciation is shown in parentheses after the _____ word.

4. Pronunciation marks are explained in a _____ at the bottom of the page.

5. In addition to pronunciation, syllables to be _____ are marked.

19 VD for the Millions

by Reg Parrish

Vocabulary—The five words below are from the story you are about to read. Study the words and their meanings. Then complete the ten sentences that follow, using one of the five words to fill in the blank in each sentence. Mark your answer by writing the letter of the word on the line before the sentence. Check your answers in the Answer Key on page 108.

A. divergent: differing

B. insidiously: subtly but harmfully

C. disseminating: spreading

D. divulge: reveal

E. licentious: sexually unrestrained

_____ 1. Doctors should take an active role in _____ information about VD.

_____ 2. Many people are reluctant to _____ the names of past sexual partners.

_____ 3. The _____ behavior of Columbus's men may have led them to contract VD from natives of the New World.

_____ 4. Different groups of people have _____ views of what constitutes proper behavior.

_____ 5. There are several _____ theories about how best to stop the current epidemic of VD.

_____ 6. In pregnant women, VD works _____, often crippling unborn babies.

_____ 7. _____ acts put a person at risk for contracting VD.

_____ 8. The author decided to _____ the news that Pope Julius II suffered from VD.

_____ 9. If untreated, VD spreads _____ through a person's body.

_____ 10. Perhaps schools should take an active role in _____ facts about VD.

You can have it. Your children can have it. It is a disease, not a sin.

The incidences of venereal diseases—gonorrhea and syphilis—are now epidemic in this country, medically one of the most advanced nations in the world. *Epidemic!* That means that venereal diseases are growing at a rate that is out of control. That means that the chances of infection are open to *everyone*—not just a few.

Yet the terrible myth persists: Nice people don't get VD. And it is this myth which continues to undercut effective programs of control. It is this myth which continues to lead to women becoming sterile and to babies being born blind, crippled, and dead. It is this myth which helps, in part, to assure that 2,500,000 people in the United States will contract gonorrhea in one year alone! It is the myth which allows us to have a new case of VD every 15 seconds!

The fact is that "nice" people do get VD. Children get it. Old people get it. The poor and the rich get it. The blacks and the whites. According to the Surgeon General of the United States Public Health Service, "Venereal Disease has become the number one communicable disease in this country, exceeded only by the common cold." That is a truly remarkable statement! It means that more people get VD than they do measles, mumps, infectious hepatitis, or mononucleosis!

To say that "nice people don't get VD is to actually say that "nice" people don't have sexual experiences, since sexual activity (particularly intercourse) is the primary method of infection. (Actually, VD can be contracted via nonsexual ways, but these incidences are rare, except for cases of congenital syphilis.)

Yet to how many people whom we normally term as "nice" do we deny the right to sexual expression? We worry about our children involving themselves with sexual experimentation, yet we don't deny that they have sexual drives. We agree that sex is best in marriage, yet we don't believe that non-marrieds are forever chaste. What the myth really says is that if a "nice" person engages in sex, he or she should avoid VD by virtue of "niceness" itself. And that kind of thinking leads to fresh epidemics.

Witness the following: Dr. Jay Schamberg, a noted Philadelphia dermatologist, reported an epidemic of teenage syphilis that was spread one evening by young people engaging in a common kissing game. Should Spin-the-Bottle now be outlawed? Should the kids who played the game be stripped forever of their label as "nice" kids? Or should some better rational thinking prevail?

The point is that there *is* a difference between "sin" and disease, between morality and treatment. "Sin" is a theo-logical concept which is widely divergent between peoples of varying faiths; disease is a physical fact requiring positive treatment. Yet the myth insidiously links the two together:

Be "nice" and you should feel ashamed—so ashamed that you will never tell anyone you have it.

The VD epidemic will not decrease until we have successfully destroyed the myth. *Anyone can and may get VD.* It is a disease just like TB is a disease, or rheumatic fever, or diabetes. No more, no less. Happily, it responds to treatment much better than many other "acceptable" diseases.

Only poor misguided people get VD? Then to the list we would have to add Pope Julius II, Fyodor Dostoyevsky, Honore de Balzac, Napoleon, Scott Joplin, and Walt Whitman. They all had it. Of course, we would also have to list Cesare Borgia and Al Capone. Clearly, VD is not a respecter of position and/or accomplishment.

Origins

Many scholars believe that Columbus discovered much more than the New World: they believe that his trips were responsible for importing syphilis to Europe. It is known that his sailors dallied with the natives, and that their return to Spain coincided with what is largely regarded as the first documented report of syphilis.

In 1504, a Spanish physician named Ruy Diaz de l'Isla reported that the pilot of Columbus's vessel came down with fever and awful skin eruptions; further, de l'Isla claimed that he had treated several sailors in Barcelona afflicted with the "new" disease.

To this day, syphilis is sometimes referred to as the "French disease." This legacy is the result of the French invasion of Naples in 1495, whereby the Italians were first visited with the ravages of syphilis which they immediately termed as *morbus gallicus* (French sickness). Not to be undone, the French countered by calling the disease *le mal de Naples* (the Naples' sickness) when the French troops returned from Italy and began spreading it among their own citizens.

The Columbus theory appears quite valid owing to the fact that very few pre-Columbian bones showing signs of possible syphilitic lesions have been discovered in Europe with a dating prior to 1493; many such bones have been found in pre-Columbian America.

Syphilis as the name of a disease did not come into being until 1521. At that time, an Italian physician of wide learning named Girolamo Fracastoro wrote a didactic poem titled *Syphilis, sive de morbus gallicus.* He described the new disease in verse and outlined various cures, notably mercury, a treatment which persisted right through to the invention of pencillin in 1928. Fracastoro took the name from the legend of Syphilus, the Greek shepherd whom Apollo inflicted with terrible boils as punishment for wrongful worship.

Gonorrhea does not have as interesting a history as syphilis. It is known to have existed for ages, but its true nature was not established until the advent of modern medicine.

The Story Today

An estimated 540,000 people in the United States have undetected syphilis today. Add the 2,500,000 new cases of gonorrhea, and it becomes plain that more than three million people will experience VD in the United States during this coming year.

Today, there are slightly more than four million 15-year-olds in the nation. At the current rate of VD infection, it is estimated that these four million young people will have *shared* more than three million cases of syphilis and gonorrhea by the time they are twenty-five! And the rate of infection for this age group has increased each year for the past six years.

In dollars alone, the direct cost of VD to the United States is $145 million a year.

Other nations are also experiencing a drastic rise in VD, but few on the order of the epidemic in America. This is largely explained by the fact that other nations, not burdened with carryovers of the "Puritan ethic," are much more frank in treating VD and in disseminating knowledge on the subject.

It is odd that generations of United States parents have passed down frequently the supposed horrors of masturbation to their children—blindness, crippling, loss of hair, etc.—but have never discussed the taboo subject of VD. While masturbation is not known to be physically harmful in the least, the results popularly ascribed to it are the very real results of syphilis! Somehow, the thinking must be changed.

Stopping the Epidemic

The sad thing about the present VD epidemic is that it need not exist. In fact, doctors a few years ago were hopeful that syphilis was about to vanish from this country; now it has returned at a greater rate than ever.

Both syphilis and gonorrhea respond magnificently to treatment by penicillin. *It is virtually unnecessary for anyone to suffer the full ravages of either syphilis or gonorrhea— both are fully curable.* The only thing that is needed is treatment. At the very first sign of either disease, a person should seek immediate medical aid. All information regarding VD is treated confidentially, always, and public health clinics will provide free treatment fully for all those needing it. Women should always request that a gonorrhea smear be taken at each checkup, and should request such a test whenever exposure to the disease is suspected. There is no immunity to the disease.

Likewise, men should see doctors at the first sign of VD, or if they suspect exposure. The earlier the treatment begins, the sooner the cure.

All states require that victims of VD divulge confidential information requiring possible sources of contact. This is necessary for proper follow-up to control the disease. Regrettably, many private physicians do not demand this information of their patients, and it is estimated that more than a million-and-a-half cases of VD go unchecked per year because of this negligent practice.

VD will only cease when the "hush-hush" aura surrounding the diseases are eliminated. And this will only come about through public instruction and worthwhile propaganda. What is needed desperately is a national program of sound VD education, particularly to young people. Plain talk is the greatest weapon against VD.

Abstinence from intimate sexual contact is the best preventive for VD. While educational programs should mention this fact, it is not realistic to build entire VD programs around it. While sexual abstinence for unmarrieds has been promulgated by all major religions, the history of the world proves that the population-at-large has never followed this particular dictum of its own preaching. Sex, whether one approves or not, and whether within marriage or without, is here to stay. But VD need not remain. It is difficult to believe that syphilis is some sort of divine curse for sexual knowledge since the majority of the world's peoples were spared it for so many ages. (Unless one believes that the natives of South America and the West Indies were singled out providentially for their licentious transgressions.)

No. VD *can* go. VD *must* go. The answer lies in truth and facts; not self-righteous sermons and mountainous shame. Morality is the concern of the individual and his conscience; public health is the concern of society. Today, that health is threatened gravely by the spiraling VD epidemic. Only society can stop that epidemic through honest education and unashamed concern. Disease is not the province of guilt.

Starting Time		Finishing Time	
Reading Time		Reading Rate	
Comprehension		Vocabulary	

Comprehension— Read the following questions and statements. For each one, put an *x* in the box before the option that contains the most complete or accurate answer. Check your answers in the Answer Key on page 108.

1. The effects of venereal disease can be
   - ☐ a. gonorrhea and syphilis.
   - ☐ b. infectious hepatitis.
   - ☐ c. mononucleosis.
   - ☐ d. deformity and death.

2. Venereal disease in the United States is a
   - ☐ a. threat to poor people.
   - ☐ b. problem for the uneducated masses.
   - ☐ c. problem of national proportions.
   - ☐ d. menace to teenagers.

3. Veneral diseases do not
   - ☐ a. attack poor, misguided people.
   - ☐ b. produce feelings of shame.
   - ☐ c. cause fever and skin eruptions.
   - ☐ d. respect social position.

4. Syphilis and gonorrhea could be effectively controlled if
   - ☐ a. people practiced self-discipline.
   - ☐ b. medicine discovered a cure.
   - ☐ c. social attitudes changed.
   - ☐ d. laws were strictly enforced.

5. Evidence seems to indicate that syphilis originated in
   - ☐ a. the New World.   ☐ c. France.
   - ☐ b. the European slums.   ☐ d. Italy.

6. Sin is to disease as
   - ☐ a. abstract is to concrete.
   - ☐ b. morality is to immorality.
   - ☐ c. knowledge is to ignorance.
   - ☐ d. prevention is to cure.

7. The "nice" people referred to in the selection are
   - ☐ a. poor.
   - ☐ b. rich.
   - ☐ c. respectable.
   - ☐ d. young.

8. The tone of the selection is
   - ☐ a. inflammatory.
   - ☐ b. embarrassed.
   - ☐ c. frank.
   - ☐ d. argumentative.

9. The author believes that venereal disease is
   - ☐ a. punishment for sexual sins.
   - ☐ b. little more than an inconvenience.
   - ☐ c. evidence of a morally corrupt society.
   - ☐ d. nothing to be ashamed of.

10. The selection is written in the form of
   - ☐ a. a critique.
   - ☐ b. a report.
   - ☐ c. an autobiography.
   - ☐ d. a dialogue.

Comprehension Skills

1. recalling specific facts	6. making a judgment
2. retaining concepts	7. making an inference
3. organizing facts	8. recognizing tone
4. understanding the main idea	9. understanding characters
5. drawing a conclusion	10. appreciation of literary forms

Study Skills, Part One—Following is a passage with blanks where words have been omitted. Next to the passage are groups of five words, one group for each blank. Complete the passage by selecting the correct word for each of the blanks.

Understanding Dictionaries, III

4. Parts of Speech. Following the pronunciation, an abbreviation or letter in italics will be used to show the part of speech. In the case of *rhythm*, the letter *n.* tells the reader that the word is a ___(1)___ . When a word can be used as more than one part of speech, a second italic abbreviation will appear later on in the entry before the definition is given for that ___(2)___ . A bold dash (-) will appear before a second part-of-speech listing.

5. Inflected Forms. Inflections are changes in spelling

(1)		place		verb
	name		noun	number

(2)		entry		usage
	unit		word	syllable

which occur in words because of plural form, verb tense, comparison of adjectives, and so on. Inflected forms come next in the entry. If a word forms a plural in an ___(3)___ way, like *mouse* and *mice,* the plural spelling is shown. Correct plural spellings for other words that cause ___(4)___ , such as *mothers-in-law* and *cupfuls,* are also given.

Inflected forms of adjectives are often given. Following *heavy,* the reader will find *heavier, heaviest;* after *good,* all dictionaries list *better, best.* For irregular verbs, like *run,* the irregular forms *(ran, run,* and *running)* are given.

6. Definitions. The definitions for a word are ___(5)___ . While many dictionaries list the most common or latest meaning for a word first, some dictionaries give definitions in ___(6)___ order. This means that the *latest* definition for a word will appear last. You should find out which system your book uses. Idiomatic or slang uses of a word are sometimes given. Following the definitions for the word *sack,* for example, you may find the ___(7)___ *hit the sack* and *sack out* listed and defined.

(3)	unusual		objective
	additional	usable	ordinary

(4)	confidence		comprehension
	correction	confusion	completion

(5)	remembered		omitted
	offered	numbered	confused

(6)	historical		sequential
	numerical	random	traditional

(7)	answers		questions
	expressions	attempts	evaluations

Study Skills, Part Two—Read the study skills passage again, paying special attention to the lesson being taught. Then, without looking back at the passage, complete each sentence below by writing in the missing word or words. Check the Answer Key on page 108 for the answers to Study Skills, Part One, and Study Skills, Part Two.

1. After the _____ is given, an italicized letter indicates the part of speech.

2. Changes in spelling for plural forms and changes in verb tense are

   called _____ .

3. Included in the above category is also the comparison of _____ .

4. The most currently used definition of a word is listed first or

   _____ .

5. Idiomatic or _____ uses of a word are sometimes given after the

   definition.

The Evidence Store

by David Owen

Vocabulary—The five words below are from the story you are about to read. Study the words and their meanings. Then complete the ten sentences that follow, using one of the five words to fill in the blank in each sentence. Mark your answer by writing the letter of the word on the line before the sentence. Check your answers in the Answer Key on page 108.

A. deterioration: the lowering or impairing of quality

B. vengeance: punishing another for a wrong he or she committed

C. compelling: forceful; demanding attention

D. exasperated: made angrily; irritated

E. agonizing: to be in extreme physical or emotional pain

_____ 1. Appelbaum's equipment helps lawyers highlight their clients' _____ injuries.

_____ 2. Appelbaum did not find selling cameras to be _____ work.

_____ 3. Lawyers often need to show how much physical _____ their clients have suffered.

_____ 4. Appelbaum found photographing fire damage and traffic accidents _____ .

_____ 5. Appelbaum's equipment makes it possible for victims to gain a measure of _____ in court.

_____ 6. As a teenager, Appelbaum was _____ by the usual routine of summer camp.

_____ 7. The man with the scar on his face wanted financial _____ for his disfigurement.

_____ 8. A herniated disk sounds like an _____ condition.

_____ 9. The _____ of someone's bones can be shown using Appelbaum's exhibits.

_____ 10. A non-lawyer visiting The Evidence Store could easily become _____ trying to figure out what's going on.

The customer was looking for something in a herniated disk. He wanted some inflammation—but not too much inflammation—and some agonizing pressure on the spinal cord. You know the kind of agonizing pressure I mean? Down in the lumbar region? He wanted it right away.

Fortunately, Stephen Appelbaum had just the thing. He carries a full line of herniated disks, some with complete prolapses and some without. His deluxe model, which costs $75, was exactly what the customer was looking for. It comes with two vertebrae, three interchangeable disks in different stages of deterioration, and a viewing stand. The customer took it with him.

Appelbaum is the proprietor of The Evidence Store, in Union, New Jersey, just west of Newark International Airport. He likes to describe his business as "the only full-service walk-in retail store for trial lawyers" and "Toys R Us for attorneys." He sells and rents not only detailed plastic models of herniated disks (his most popular item) but also models of pelvises, legs, jaws, hearts, knees, eyes (two sizes), spines, wrists, shoulders (from five different manufacturers), hands, brains, and other body parts. Lawyers use the models to create compelling courtroom exhibits in personal-injury lawsuits.

Appelbaum also sells a lot of things, including a full-color poster called "Normal female abdominal anatomy post CO_2 gas insufflation," scale models of traffic accidents, coffee cups covered with humorous sayings about the legal profession, The People's Court board game, a set of false teeth called Mr. Gross Mouth (which has fake gum disease and spits real tobacco juice), bumper stickers that say MY LAWYER CAN BEAT UP YOUR LAWYER (these are free), and a diagram illustrating that standby of the personal-injury trade, "whiplash cervical misalignment."

A typical Evidence Store customer is a lawyer from Newark whose attempt to settle his client's $20 million medical-malpractice suit for $40,000 has just collapsed. He now finds himself going to trial with nothing to show the jury. So he calls Appelbaum or, as often happens, drops in to browse. If he has a carpal-tunnel-syndrome case, Appelbaum may sell him a model of a wrist that a surgeon can dissect in front of the jury. If he's representing a woman who fell off a barstool and hit her head on a cigarette machine, Appelbaum may rent him a halo traction brace with a padded plastic jacket, so the jury can get an idea of what it's like to have a broken neck. If the lawyer plans to introduce an X-ray as evidence, Appelbaum may suggest making a dramatic enlargement. One such enlargement, depicting the bones in someone's leg, is tacked to a door in The Evidence Store. The bones

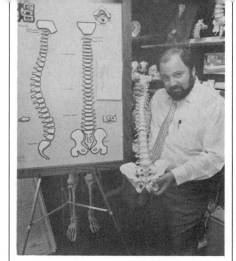

He describes his business as "the only full-service walk-in retail store for trial lawyers" and "Toys R Us for attorneys."

are held together by eight screws and a metal plate. Written in black ink at the top of the picture is "$350,000!!!"

Every now and then a curious non-lawyer will spot Appelbaum's sign and wander in to find out what a store called The Evidence Store could possibly sell. Appelbaum likes to kid around with these people. He tells them, "Figure out what we do and win a prize." They look at the skinless leg model. They look at the sign that says YOUR SPINAL CORD INJURY . . . WHAT HAPPENS TO BLADDER AND BOWEL CONTROL? They look at the X-ray of a bullet lodged in a spine. They look at the mildly pornographic light-switch plates (popular with legal secretaries, who often shop for their bosses). Then they give up.

Stephen Appelbaum didn't grow up wanting to sell copies of The Slip and Fall Handbook to lawyers in eastern New Jersey. In fact, in the early 1960s, as a grumpy teenager attending summer camp in Nyack, New York, he didn't want to do anything at all. He didn't like sports. He didn't like outdoor activities of any kind. His exasperated counselor—the novelist Chaim Potok, incidentally—suggested that he take up photography. This he did with a vengeance, returning to camp the following summer with his own portable darkroom, which he set up in his bunk.

After earning a degree in photographic illustration at the Rochester Institute of Technology, Appelbaum held a number of jobs that involved either taking pictures or selling cameras. Nothing captured his imagination, though, until his cousin, an insurance-claims adjuster, called him one day and asked if he'd like to photograph some fire damage. Appelbaum found that he enjoyed photographing fire damage. In time he branched out into traffic accidents.

Soon Appelbaum was receiving inquiries from lawyers who had seen his fire-damage and traffic-accident pictures in courtrooms and wanted him to photograph bungled face-lifts and slippery floors. His business grew. In addition to taking pictures, he began blowing up X-rays and medical charts. Then he began selling easels to hold the enlargements. Then he began selling cases to hold the enlargements and the easels. Then he heard from a friend who had just opened a skeleton-rental service in Atlanta. A pretty nutty idea, renting skeletons—but didn't lawyers sometimes need skeletons? He bought a full-sized plastic skeleton and named it Fred.

Except when he's rented out, Fred still stands in a prominent place inside The Evidence Store. When I visited, not long ago, Fred was smoking a pipe and wearing a leather cap, sunglasses, a skeleton necklace, and a red T-shirt that said I'M FRED . . . TAKE ME TO COURT. Beside him was another skeleton, also for rent. Two days before, Appelbaum had sold a deluxe skeleton (all the bones numbered, muscle origins painted in red and blue) for just under $1,300. The skeletons are shipped in big cardboard boxes that look like coffins.

Taking pictures of other people's misfortunes is still a key source of income for Appelbaum and his three assistants. (Their photographic business is called Garden State Legal Photo Service.) Appelbaum does much of his photographic work in a cluttered studio that adjoins, and occasionally overflows into, The Evidence Store.

"You should have been here a couple of weeks ago," he told me. "I had one guy who had been beaten up by the cops, and another guy who had what they call an external fixation device. All his bones were being held together from the outside, with all these pins going through his leg. So he's sitting here, and over there is some other guy with crutches and lacerations and scabs. It looked like a hospital waiting room. Next!"

"I've got a big problem," Appelbaum told me. "I happen to enjoy what I do." One thing Appelbaum particularly enjoys about his work is the occasional opportunity it gives him to emulate his hero, Paul Drake. You remember Paul Drake—the private detective who works with Perry Mason. Paul Drake is always rushing into the courtroom just before the end of the show. Perry Mason says, "May I have a moment, Your Honor?" Then Paul Drake whispers something into his ear and hands him a little piece of paper. Perry Mason steps up to the witness stand and reads from the little piece of paper. When the witness hears whatever is written on the paper, he falls into a fit of lunatic sobbing and blurts out a detailed confession of the crime.

Of course, everyone knows that the legal process doesn't really work like that. Most cases don't even get to court, or if they do, they tend not to stay there very long. My wife once served on a jury in a case that ended in a plea-bargain after the defense attorney inadvertently referred to his client, in front of the jury, as "Mr. Guilty." Next!

You can never tell how things are going to go at The Evidence Store. Some days are slow. On slow days Appelbaum's assistants tend to spend a lot of time going out for coffee and forgetting to remind Appelbaum to pick up his nine-year-old daughter, Carly, at school. But other days are filled with action. Recently Appelbaum had to go out and crawl around in some muddy, rat-infested tunnels under the foundation of a new building. The ground under the foundation had been sinking. Appelbaum's job was to take pictures of broken pipes and electrical connections. ("I felt like I was escaping from Nazi Germany. With camera equipment.") Over the weekend he had taken pictures at a lake where someone had dived off the end of a dock into two feet of water and become a quadriplegic.

Appelbaum doesn't think much of the dramatic instincts of most lawyers. In preparing a case, he believes, your typical lawyer will spend many months piling up and poring over thousands of documents and deposing dozens of witnesses. The photocopying bill alone would be enough to put many people in the poorhouse. When the case comes to trial, the lawyer will scrutinize potential jurors and attempt scientifically to weed out those who might have a predilection for not awarding millions of dollars to people who stumble or get stumbled upon. Then, with all the pieces finally in place, the lawyer will use the months of careful preparation and the mountain of photocopied documents to put the scientifically selected jury to sleep.

"The law by tradition is a profession of words and abstract ideas," Appelbaum told me. "It's not visually oriented, and lawyers aren't trained in law school to work in the courtroom."

Appelbaum tries to teach lawyers what law school didn't. If the case hinges on a few crucial documents, he may suggest copying them and placing the copies in attractive binders, so that the jury can follow along. (The ideal number of binders, according to Appelbaum, is half the number of jurors; sharing helps people stay awake.) If the case involves crippling injuries, he may suggest making a day-in-the-life videotape to show how much trouble the plaintiff has tying his shoes and combing his hair. (The idea length of a day-in-the-life videotape, according to Appelbaum, is twenty minutes—roughly the length of a half-hour television show minus the commercials.)

Walking into a courtroom and seeing a movie projector, Appelbaum told me, produces in a juror a feeling of elation that should be familiar to anyone who ever attended school. Yet few lawyers take advantage of this powerful human emotion. Some seem to forget about the jury altogether. One reason companies lose big lawsuits, according to a recent article in *The New York Times,* is that they are "represented by obnoxious counsel."

Appelbaum is trying to help. He has invented a magnetic display board, called the Mini-Map, that lawyers, police officers, and others can use to reconstruct traffic accidents. The Mini-Map, which sells for $100 (including magnetic cars, marking pens, a drawing template, and a carrying case), was recently featured in the new-products section of the *Cincinnati Court Index.*

Several people have even approached Appelbaum recently about franchising The Evidence Store nationwide. Soon you may not have to go all the way to Union, New Jersey, to rent a leg. Trials could eventually become so interesting that people might refuse to settle out of court, simply for fear of missing the movie.

Starting Time			*Finishing Time*	
Reading Time			*Reading Rate*	
Comprehension			*Vocabulary*	

Comprehension— Read the following questions and statements. For each one, put an *x* in the box before the option that contains the most complete or accurate answer. Check your answers in the Answer Key on page 108.

1. Lawyers use Appelbaum's models in cases involving
   ☐ a. slander.
   ☐ b. murder.
   ☐ c. personal injury.
   ☐ d. breach of contract.

2. A major change in Appelbaum's life occurred when he developed an interest in
   ☐ a. photography.
   ☐ b. medicine.
   ☐ c. baseball.
   ☐ d. hiking.

3. Before earning his degree, Appelbaum
   ☐ a. rented skeletons.
   ☐ b. opened The Evidence Store.
   ☐ c. photographed traffic accidents.
   ☐ d. bought a portable darkroom.

4. The main point of the story is to show how Appelbaum
   ☐ a. meets the needs of lawyers.
   ☐ b. reacted to his summer-camp experience.
   ☐ c. decorates his store.
   ☐ d. became a very funny man.

5. Appelbaum finds his work
   ☐ a. frustrating.
   ☐ b. morally uplifting.
   ☐ c. repetitive.
   ☐ d. enjoyable.

6. The chief reason lawyers use Appelbaum's devices is to
   ☐ a. save on expenses.
   ☐ b. influence the judge.
   ☐ c. amuse themselves.
   ☐ d. interest the jury.

7. The lawyers who use Appelbaum's models are motivated by
   ☐ a. profit.
   ☐ b. a sense of justice.
   ☐ c. moral indignation.
   ☐ d. deep personal grief.

8. Appelbaum decorated his store like a
   ☐ a. joke shop.
   ☐ b. fast-food restaurant.
   ☐ c. drugstore.
   ☐ d. funeral parlor.

9. Appelbaum seems to be
   ☐ a. a frustrated, would-be lawyer.
   ☐ b. an off-beat, humorous man.
   ☐ c. a man easily moved by human tragedy.
   ☐ d. angry at the world.

10. The opening sentence about a customer looking "for something in a herniated disk" is intended to
    ☐ a. inform the reader.
    ☐ b. mislead the reader.
    ☐ c. intrigue the reader.
    ☐ d. amuse the reader.

Comprehension Skills	
1. recalling specific facts	6. making a judgment
2. retaining concepts	7. making an inference
3. organizing facts	8. recognizing tone
4. understanding the main idea	9. understanding characters
5. drawing a conclusion	10. appreciation of literary forms

Study Skills, Part One—Following is a passage with blanks where words have been omitted. Next to the passage are groups of five words, one group for each blank. Complete the passage by selecting the correct word for each of the blanks.

Understanding Dictionaries, IV

7. Restrictive Labels. When a definition pertains to a certain subject field, an abbreviated label will show before it. In printing circles, the word *face* refers to a design or style of type. In the dictionary, this meaning is given along with the others, but it is ___(1)___ by the restrictive label, *Print*.

(1) replaced   succeeded
     followed   preceded   interrupted

In England, a word may have a __(2)__ meaning. The dictionary would show *Brit.* before it. Restrictive labels are also used to indicate *Slang* or *Informal* usages and definitions.

8. Etymologies. The history or derivation of a word is given. It may appear before the definitions or it may follow them. The etymology is shown in square brackets; it tells the reader the language a word comes from and also its spelling in that language. Useful information about the __(3)__ and meanings of the roots and affixes of a word can also be found with the etymology.

9. Run-on Entries. Near the end of the entry, derivative forms are listed. These forms are __(4)__ in words caused by the addition of suffixes. Accordingly, following *gradual,* you can expect to find *gradually* and *gradualness* listed.

10. Synonyms. For certain common words, dictionaries show synonyms, words with the same or nearly the same meaning as the __(5)__ word. Synonyms usually appear following the entry, at the left margin, preceded by the abbreviation *Syn.* Antonyms, words with opposite __(6)__ , may be given after the synonyms. These would also appear at the left margin and be preceded by the abbreviation *Ant.*

11. Contextual Illustrations. Every dictionary uses words in context to help make meanings clear. These appear as brief phrases, although occasionally complete sentences may be given. The usages indicate how the entry word can be used and how its meaning __(7)__ in context.

(2)   difficult   similar   special   senseless   formal

(3)   origins   contexts   pronunciations   inflections   uses

(4)   changes   improvements   inflections   contradictions   complications

(5)   new   entry   preceding   following   foreign

(6)   appearances   spellings   pronunciations   meanings   histories

(7)   remains   sounds   varies   looks   functions

Study Skills, Part Two—Read the study skills passage again, paying special attention to the lesson being taught. Then, without looking back at the passage, complete each sentence below by writing in the missing word or words. Check the Answer Key on page 108 for the answers to Study Skills, Part One, and Study Skills, Part Two.

1. Restrictive labels are used to show that a definition pertains to a certain _____ field.

2. The history or derivation of a word, called the _____ , is shown in square brackets.

3. Changes in words by the addition of various endings are called _____ forms.

4. Words meaning the same or the opposite of the defined words are called synonyms and _____ , respectively.

5. Defined words are shown in _____ to show how the words can be used.

Answer Key

Selection 1

Vocabulary
1. B   6. B
2. C   7. E
3. E   8. A
4. A   9. D
5. D   10. C

Comprehension
1. b   6. b
2. a   7. b
3. d   8. a
4. c   9. c
5. c   10. d

Study Skills, Part One
1. seeing   6. Inaccurate
2. words   7. missed
3. print
4. rapid
5. smooth

Study Skills, Part Two
1. reading
2. fixation
3. unaware
4. beginning
5. regressions

Selection 2

Vocabulary
1. C   6. C
2. E   7. A
3. D   8. E
4. A   9. D
5. B   10. B

Comprehension
1. c   6. c
2. a   7. a
3. b   8. a
4. a   9. c
5. a   10. d

Study Skills, Part One
1. fewer   6. sense
2. indications 7. silently
3. accurate
4. combining
5. spoken

Study Skills, Part Two
1. fixations
2. improvement
3. meaning
4. oral
5. context

Selection 3

Vocabulary
1. C   6. E
2. D   7. D
3. A   8. C
4. E   9. A
5. B   10. B

Comprehension
1. b   6. d
2. a   7. b
3. c   8. d
4. b   9. d
5. b   10. b

Study Skills, Part One
1. comprehen-   5. printed
   sion   6. sounds
2. written   7. important
3. word
4. pronunciation

Study Skills, Part Two
1. association
2. listening
3. Phonics
4. printed
5. vowels

Selection 4

Vocabulary
1. E   6. E
2. B   7. A
3. D   8. C
4. C   9. A
5. D   10. B

Comprehension
1. c   6. a
2. b   7. a
3. c   8. b
4. c   9. b
5. d   10. c

Study Skills, Part One
1. vowels   6. recognize
2. letter   7. practice
3. reading
4. sounding
5. stumbling

Study Skills, Part Two
1. language
2. skills
3. sight
4. enjoy
5. mental

Selection 5

Vocabulary
1. B   6. E
2. A   7. B
3. E   8. A
4. C   9. D
5. D   10. C

Comprehension
1. c   6. b
2. a   7. b
3. d   8. d
4. c   9. c
5. d   10. c

Study Skills, Part One
1. selective   6. patterns
2. sentences   7. recognizing
3. key
4. flexible
5. techniques

Study Skills, Part Two
1. thought
2. main idea
3. details
4. ideas
5. skills

Selection 6

Vocabulary
1. B   6. E
2. D   7. D
3. C   8. C
4. A   9. E
5. B   10. A

Comprehension
1. c   6. a
2. c   7. b
3. c   8. c
4. d   9. c
5. d   10. b

Study Skills, Part One
1. paragraph   6. recognizes
2. illustrate   7. important
3. Typically
4. administration
5. sympathetic

Study Skills, Part Two
1. story
2. moral
3. psychology
4. end
5. story

Selection 7

Vocabulary

1. A	6. E
2. E	7. B
3. D	8. D
4. B	9. C
5. C	10. A

Comprehension

1. c	6. c
2. a	7. d
3. b	8. d
4. b	9. c
5. a	10. d

Study Skills, Part One

1. salesperson   6. infor-
2. pitch   mation
3. truth   7. critically
4. blotter
5. standard

Study Skills, Part Two

1. details
2. main idea
3. think
4. judge
5. relate

Selection 8

Vocabulary

1. A	6. D
2. E	7. B
3. C	8. C
4. B	9. D
5. A	10. E

Comprehension

1. a	6. b
2. a	7. c
3. b	8. d
4. a	9. d
5. c	10. b

Study Skills, Part One

1. successive   6. conclusion
2. premises   7. validity
3. practice
4. wasteful
5. schools

Study Skills, Part Two

1. persuasion
2. leading
3. habits
4. alternative
5. valid

Selection 9

Vocabulary

1. E	6. E
2. A	7. B
3. C	8. D
4. A	9. D
5. C	10. B

Comprehension

1. c	6. a
2. a	7. d
3. c	8. b
4. a	9. d
5. d	10. c

Study Skills, Part One

1. builds   6. progress
2. general   7. broad
3. certain
4. knows
5. generalization

Study Skills, Part Two

1. lesser
2. developed
3. nothing
4. inclusive
5. concept

Selection 10

Vocabulary

1. B	6. C
2. D	7. E
3. A	8. A
4. E	9. C
5. B	10. D

Comprehension

1. c	6. c
2. d	7. b
3. d	8. a
4. a	9. a
5. c	10. d

Study Skills, Part One

1. inversion   6. anecdote
2. frustrates   7. retain
3. information
4. talking
5. require

Study Skills, Part Two

1. beginning
2. end
3. dull
4. illustrate
5. facts

Selection 11

Vocabulary

1. A	6. B
2. C	7. A
3. D	8. E
4. E	9. B
5. C	10. D

Comprehension

1. d	6. d
2. c	7. a
3. a	8. c
4. a	9. b
5. d	10. b

Study Skills, Part One

1. supporting 6. formal
2. intellectual 7. textbooks
3. sustained
4. falters
5. perceived

Study Skills, Part Two

1. Salestalk
2. followed
3. college
4. concentration
5. examine

Selection 12

Vocabulary

1. C	6. E
2. A	7. B
3. D	8. A
4. E	9. B
5. C	10. D

Comprehension

1. d	6. d
2. c	7. b
3. c	8. c
4. c	9. b
5. a	10. a

Study Skills, Part One

1. sequential   6. shadow
2. narrows   7. evaluate
3. consciousness
4. wants
5. significance

Study Skills, Part Two

1. Therefore
2. arguments
3. awareness
4. spotlight
5. opposite

Selection 13

Vocabulary

1. B	6. A
2. A	7. E
3. D	8. D
4. C	9. B
5. E	10. C

Comprehension

1. b	6. c
2. b	7. c
3. c	8. d
4. c	9. c
5. b	10. b

Study Skills, Part One

1. those   6. continuity
2. additional   7. entice
3. distraction
4. wavering
5. danger

Study Skills, Part Two

1. middle
2. thoughts
3. presented
4. understanding
5. introductory

Selection 14

Vocabulary

1. B	6. A
2. D	7. E
3. C	8. A
4. B	9. D
5. E	10. C

Comprehension

1. d	6. a
2. d	7. c
3. b	8. b
4. c	9. b
5. a	10. b

Study Skills, Part One

1. others	6. desire
2. heading	7. automobile
3. pleasures	
4. pocketbook	
5. necessary	

Study Skills, Part Two

1. main idea
2. campus
3. against
4. time
5. transition

Selection 15

Vocabulary

1. D	6. D
2. C	7. B
3. E	8. A
4. A	9. C
5. B	10. E

Comprehension

1. b	6. d
2. b	7. a
3. b	8. c
4. a	9. c
5. c	10. b

Study Skills, Part One

1. generaliza-tion	5. pleasure
2. repeated	6. repetition
3. time	7. two
4. desire	

Study Skills, Part Two

1. ends
2. details
3. television
4. reading
5. chance

Selection 16

Vocabulary

1. D	6. A
2. E	7. B
3. C	8. E
4. B	9. C
5. A	10. D

Comprehension

1. c	6. b
2. d	7. d
3. d	8. c
4. a	9. c
5. a	10. b

Study Skills, Part One

1. appear	6. choice
2. implied	7. together
3. difficulties	
4. positive	
5. observer	

Study Skills, Part Two

1. stated
2. impression
3. doubting
4. neutrality
5. general

Selection 17

Vocabulary

1. A	6. A
2. C	7. B
3. D	8. D
4. B	9. E
5. E	10. C

Comprehension

1. b	6. d
2. c	7. d
3. a	8. d
4. a	9. a
5. c	10. a

Study Skills, Part One

1. usable	6. foreign
2. first	7. measures
3. order	
4. larger	
5. separately	

Study Skills, Part Two

1. effectively
2. sense
3. found
4. unrelated
5. encyclopedias

Selection 18

Vocabulary

1. C	6. C
2. E	7. E
3. A	8. B
4. B	9. D
5. D	10. A

Comprehension

1. c	6. b
2. c	7. c
3. b	8. b
4. b	9. a
5. b	10. c

Study Skills, Part One

1. hyphenate	6. clear
2. divided	7. indicated
3. needed	
4. common	
5. confused	

Study Skills, Part Two

1. syllables
2. between
3. entry
4. key
5. stressed

Selection 19

Vocabulary

1. C	6. B
2. D	7. E
3. E	8. D
4. A	9. B
5. A	10. C

Comprehension

1. d	6. a
2. c	7. c
3. d	8. c
4. c	9. d
5. a	10. b

Study Skills, Part One

1. noun	6. historical
2. usage	7. expressions
3. unusual	
4. confusion	
5. numbered	

Study Skills, Part Two

1. pronunciation
2. inflections
3. adjectives
4. last
5. slang

Selection 20

Vocabulary

1. E	6. D
2. C	7. B
3. A	8. E
4. C	9. A
5. B	10. D

Comprehension

1. c	6. d
2. a	7. a
3. d	8. a
4. a	9. b
5. d	10. c

Study Skills, Part One

1. preceded	6. meanings
2. special	7. varies
3. origins	
4. changes	
5. entry	

Study Skills, Part Two

1. subject
2. etymology
3. derivative
4. antonyms
5. context

Bibliography

Every effort has been made to locate the author, publisher, place of publication, and copyright date for each selection.

Barber, James David. "The Fight to Stop Torture." In *USA Today* magazine. Valley Stream, New York: Society for the Advancement of Education, 1987.

Carter, Betty W. "The Return of the Salmon."

Cuomo, Mario M. "Preserving Freedom of the Press." In *USA Today* magazine. Valley Stream, New York: Society for the Advancement of Education, 1986.

Diamond, Eva. "Travels with Ichabod." In *Motorland.* California State Automobile Association, 1972.

Grant, Eleanor. "The Exercise Fix." In *Psychology Today.* Washington, DC: American Psychological Association, 1988.

Keats, John. "The Great American Vandal." In *Travel & Leisure.* New York: American Express Publishing Corporation, 1972.

Kubler-Ross, Dr. Elizabeth. "Death with Dignity."

Kuralt, Charles. "Something's Happening Out There." In *Family Circle* magazine. Family Circle Magazine, 1973.

Matthews, Downs. "Preserving Alaska's Prehistory." In *Exxon USA.* Exxon Company.

Maine, C. E. "Hiroshima—Death and Rebirth." In *50 True Tales of Horror.* Edited by John Canning. Century Books, Ltd., 1972.

McClure, Stanley W. "Lincoln's Last Day."

Olesky, Walter. "Tell-Tale Stones, Old Bones." In *Marathon World.* Marathon Oil Company.

Owen, David. "The Evidence Store." In *Atlantic Monthly.* Boston: The Atlantic Monthly Company, 1988.

Parrish, Reg. "VD for the Millions." In *Future* magazine. United States Jaycees.

Peter, Dr. Lawrence J., and Raymond Hull. *The Peter Principle.* New York: William Morrow & Company, 1969.

Shelton, William. "Winning the Battle of the Bug." In *Exxon USA.* Exxon Company.

"The Day Man First Flew."

Words per Minute

Selection	20	19	18	17	16	15	14	13	12	11	10	9	8	7	6	5	4	3	2	1
No. of Words	1825	1665	1950	1885	1650	1845	1875	1580	1380	1855	2255	2015	1760	1410	1375	1655	1810	1625	1520	1585
1:20	1370	1250	1460	1415	1240	1385	1405	1185	1035	1390	1690	1510	1320	1055	1030	1240	1360	1220	1140	1190
1:40	1095	1000	1170	1130	990	1105	1125	950	830	1115	1355	1210	1055	845	825	995	1085	975	910	950
2:00	910	830	975	940	825	920	940	790	690	930	1130	1010	880	705	690	830	905	810	760	790
2:20	780	715	835	810	705	790	805	675	590	795	965	865	755	605	590	710	775	695	650	680
2:40	685	625	730	705	620	690	705	590	520	695	845	755	660	530	515	620	680	610	570	595
3:00	610	555	650	630	550	615	625	525	460	620	750	670	585	470	460	550	605	540	505	530
3:20	550	500	585	565	495	555	560	475	415	555	675	605	530	425	410	495	545	490	455	475
3:40	500	455	530	515	450	505	510	430	375	505	615	550	480	385	375	450	495	445	415	430
4:00	455	415	490	470	410	460	470	395	345	465	565	505	440	350	345	415	450	405	380	395
4:20	420	385	450	435	380	425	435	365	320	430	520	465	405	325	315	380	420	375	350	365
4:40	390	355	420	405	355	395	400	340	295	400	485	430	375	300	295	355	390	350	325	340
5:00	365	335	390	375	330	370	375	315	275	370	450	405	350	280	275	330	360	325	305	315
5:20	340	310	365	355	310	345	350	295	260	350	425	380	330	265	260	310	340	305	285	295
5:40	320	295	345	335	290	325	330	280	245	325	400	355	310	250	245	290	320	285	270	280
6:00	305	280	325	315	275	310	310	265	230	310	375	335	295	235	230	275	300	270	255	265
6:20	290	265	310	300	260	290	295	250	220	295	355	320	280	225	215	260	285	255	240	250
6:40	275	250	290	285	250	275	280	235	205	280	340	300	265	210	205	250	270	245	230	240
7:00	260	240	280	270	235	265	270	225	195	265	320	290	250	200	195	235	260	230	215	225
7:20	250	225	265	255	225	250	255	215	190	255	310	275	240	190	190	225	245	220	205	215
7:40	240	215	255	245	215	240	245	205	180	240	295	265	230	185	180	215	235	210	200	205
8:00	230	210	245	235	205	230	235	200	170	230	280	250	220	175	170	205	225	205	190	200
8:20	220	200	235	225	200	220	225	190	165	225	270	240	210	170	165	200	215	195	180	190
8:40	210	190	225	220	190	215	215	180	160	215	260	230	205	165	160	190	210	190	175	185
9:00	205	185	215	210	185	205	210	175	155	205	250	225	195	155	155	185	200	180	170	175
9:20	195	180	210	200	175	200	200	170	150	200	240	215	190	150	145	175	195	175	165	170
9:40	190	170	200	195	170	190	195	165	145	190	235	210	180	145	140	170	185	170	155	165
10:00	180	165	195	190	165	185	190	160	140	185	225	200	175	140	140	165	180	160	150	160
10:20	175	160	190	180	160	180	180	155	135	180	220	195	170	135	135	160	175	155	145	155
10:40	170	155	185	175	155	175	175	150	130	175	210	190	165	130	130	155	170	150	145	150
11:00	165	150	175	170	150	170	170	145	125	170	205	185	160	130	125	150	165	145	140	145
11:20	160	145	170	165	145	165	165	140	120	165	200	180	155	125	120	145	160	145	135	140
11:40	155	145	165	160	140	160	160	135	120	160	195	175	150	120	120	140	155	140	130	135
12:00	150	140	160	155	140	155	155	130	115	155	190	170	145	120	115	140	150	135	125	130
12:20	150	135	160	155	135	150	150	130	110	150	185	165	145	115	110	135	145	130	125	130
12:40	145	130	155	150	130	145	150	125	110	145	180	160	140	110	110	130	145	130	120	125
13:00	140	130	150	145	125	140	145	120	105	145	175	155	135	110	105	125	140	125	115	120
13:20	135	125	145	140	125	140	140	120	105	140	170	150	130	105	105	125	135	120	115	120
13:40	135	120	145	140	120	135	135	115	100	135	165	145	130	105	100	120	130	120	110	115
14:00	130	120	140	135	120	130	135	115	100	130	160	145	125	100	100	120	130	115	110	115
14:20	125	115	135	130	115	130	130	110	95	130	155	140	125	100	95	115	125	115	105	110
14:40	125	115	135	130	110	125	130	110	95	125	155	135	120	95	95	115	125	110	105	110
15:00	120	110	130	125	110	125	125	105	90	125	150	135	115	95	90	110	120	110	100	105

Minutes and Seconds Elapsed

Progress Graph

Scores

Selection	Words per Minute	100	90	80	70	60	50	40	30	20
1										
2										
3										
4										
5										
6										
7										
8										
9										
10										
11										
12										
13										
14										
15										
16										
17										
18										
19										
20										

Comprehension Skills Profile

The graph below is designed to help you see your areas of comprehension weakness. Because all the comprehension questions in this text are coded, it is possible for you to determine which kinds of questions give you the most trouble.

On the graph below, keep a record of questions you have answered incorrectly. Following each selection, darken a square on the graph next to the number of the question missed. The columns are labeled with the selection numbers.

By looking at the chart and noting the number of shaded squares, you should be able to tell which areas of comprehension you are weak in. A large number of shaded squares across from a particular skill signifies an area of reading comprehension weakness. When you discover a particular weakness, give greater attention and time to answering questions of that type.

Further, you might wish to check with your instructor for recommendations of appropriate practice materials.

Selection

Categories of Comprehension Skills	1	2	3	4	5	6	7	8	9	10	11	12	13	14	15	16	17	18	19	20
1. Recalling Specific Facts																				
2. Retaining Concepts																				
3. Organizing Facts																				
4. Understanding the Main Idea																				
5. Drawing a Conclusion																				
6. Making a Judgment																				
7. Making an Inference																				
8. Recognizing Tone																				
9. Understanding Characters																				
10. Appreciation of Literary Forms																				